Outstanding Dissertations in Bilingual Education

Recognized by the National Advisory Council on Bilingual Education, 1979

NATIONAL CLEARINGHOUSE
FOR BILINGUAL EDUCATION

This document is published by InterAmerica Research Associates, Inc., pursuant to contract NIE 400-77-0101 to operate the National Clearinghouse for Bilingual Education. The National Clearinghouse for Bilingual Education is jointly funded by the National Institute of Education and the Office of Bilingual Education and Minority Languages Affairs, U.S. Department of Education. Contractors undertaking such projects under government sponsorship are encouraged to express their judgment freely in professional and technical matters; the views expressed in this publication do not necessarily reflect the views of the sponsoring agencies.

InterAmerica Research Associates, Inc. d/b/a
National Clearinghouse for Bilingual Education
1300 Wilson Boulevard, Suite B2-11
Rosslyn, Virginia 22209
(703) 522-0710/(800) 336-4560

Library of Congress Catalog Card Number: 80-80120
ISBN: 0-89763-020-3
First printing 1980
Printed in USA

10 9 8 7 6 5 4 3 2

17894

Contents

Foreword

Outstanding Dissertations in Bilingual Education contains summaries of eight dissertations recognized by the National Advisory Council on Bilingual Education in 1979. The material presented in this book represents a growing body of diverse scholarship in the field of bilingual education.

In 1978 Alfredo de los Santos, a member of the National Advisory Council on Bilingual Education, proposed that the council recognize distinguished research in bilingual education by sponsoring an Outstanding Dissertations Competition. De los Santos and the council developed rules and procedures for the competition based on guidelines formulated by other professional organizations such as the International Reading Association, the Council of Community College Professors, and the American Psychological Association. Award winners were formally announced at the annual meeting of the National Association for Bilingual Education in Seattle, Washington, May 4-9, 1979.

One of the activities of the National Clearinghouse for Bilingual Education is to publish documents addressing the specific information needs of the bilingual education community. We are proud to add this distinguished collection of papers to our growing list of publications. Subsequent Clearinghouse products will similarly seek to contribute information and knowledge which can assist in the education of minority culture and language groups in the United States.

National Clearinghouse
for Bilingual Education

Panel of Judges, 1979
Outstanding Dissertations
National Advisory Council on Bilingual Education

Alfredo G. de los Santos, Jr.,
  Chair
Vice Chancellor for Educational
  Development
Maricopa Community College
Phoenix, Arizona

Rosalie K. Bassett
Curriculum Coordinator
Johnson-O'Malley Consortium
Toppenish, Washington

Francesco Cordasco
Montclair State College
Upper Montclair, New Jersey

Edward DeAvila
DeAvila, Duncan & Associates
Larkspur, California

Norma G. Hernández
Dean, College of Education
University of Texas at El Paso
El Paso, Texas

Luis Laosa
Division of Educational Studies
Educational Testing Service
Princeton, New Jersey

Carmen A. Pérez
Director, Bilingual Education
State Department of Education
Albany, New York

Members
of the
National Advisory Council on Bilingual Education

Paula Savino Alleva
Director, Project ABLE
Bilingual Resource Center
    at P.S. 97
Brooklyn, New York

Rosalie K. Bassett
Curriculum Coordinator
Johnson-O'Malley Consortium
Toppenish, Washington

Edward T. Costa
Deputy Assistant Commissioner
Rhode Island Department of
    Education
Providence, Rhode Island

Roberto Cruz
Executive Director
Bay Area Bilingual
    Education League
Berkeley, California

Alfredo G. de los Santos, Jr.
Vice Chancellor for Educational
    Development
Maricopa Community Colleges
Phoenix, Arizona

Robert G. Fontenot
Professor and Director
Bilingual Center
University of Southwestern
    Louisiana
Lafayette, Louisiana

Fucheng Richard Hsu
President
China Institute in America, Inc.
New York, New York

James D. Lehmann
Coordinator, Bilingual and
    Migrant Education
Education Service Center,
    Region XX
San Antonio, Texas

María C. Sánchez
Board Member
Hartford Board of Education
Hartford, Connecticut

María Medina Swanson
Director
Bilingual Education Service
    Center
Arlington Heights, Illinois

Francis T. Villemain
Dean, School of Education
San Jose State University
San Jose, California

The 1974 Bilingual Education Amendments: Revolution, Reaction, or Reform

Susan Gilbert Schneider

First Place, Outstanding Dissertations
National Advisory Council on Bilingual Education

Degree conferred December 1976
University of Maryland
College Park, Maryland

Dissertation Committee:
Janet Baird, *Chair*
Jean D. Grambs
Rudolph Troike
William E. DeLorenzo
George Male

About the Author

Dr. Susan Gilbert Schneider is a Special Assistant to the Secretary of the Department of Health, Education, and Welfare in Washington, D.C., and the Director of the Secretary's Advisory Committee Office. Dr. Schneider's dissertation, *Revolution, Reaction or Reform: The 1974 Bilingual Education Act*, was published by Las Américas of New York in 1976. Copies can be obtained for $7.95 from Las Américas Publishing Company, Inc., 37 Union Square West, New York, NY 10003, as well as from the Center for Applied Linguistics, 1611 North Kent Street, Arlington, VA 22209.

Purpose

The study examined in detail the legislative history of the 1974 Bilingual Education Act, Section 105 of the Education Amendments of 1974, Public Law 93-380. The study examined the roles of representatives, senators, lobbyists, judicial decisions, minority groups, and administration officials in developing the 1974 Bilingual Education Act.

Research Questions

A series of research questions were explored. How did the 1974 act define the appropriate federal role in meeting the needs of linguistic minorities? Did the 1974 act commit the federal government to provide direct bilingual-bicultural educational services or did it limit the federal role to secondary support? Did the 1974 act continue the transitional approach of the 1968 Bilingual Education Act or did it also permit maintenance models? What future direction did the 1974 act chart for bilingual-bicultural education? Was the 1974 act revolutionary, reactionary, or reformist?

Procedure

The researcher examined literature in the field of bilingual-bicultural education legislation. Congressional and administration documents were analyzed in this case study. Interviews were conducted with representatives and senators, congressional staff, administration officials, lobbyists, and educators involved in the legislative process. Material also included personal files permitting an understanding of the diverse strategies affecting the legislative process.

The document was organized as follows:

Chapter 1: Introduction
Chapter 2: Review of Literature
Chapter 3: History and Legislative Background of Bilingual-Bicultural Education
Chapter 4: Development of the Senate Position
Chapter 5: Development of the House Position
Chapter 6: Development of the Administration Position and Its Effect on the Legislative Process in the Senate and House
Chapter 7: The Conference and Passage
Chapter 8: Summary, Analysis, and Implications of the 1974 Bilingual Education Amendments
Selected Bibliography
Appendixes A - P

Research Findings

Senators and congressmen with large numbers of limited-English-speaking constituents echoed their constituents' support for bilingual-bicultural education. Congressional staff responsibility encompassed all aspects of the legislative process. Congressional courtesy and the personal relationships of legislators with their colleagues had a major impact on the legislative process, promoting the integration of different views of the federal role in bilingual-bicultural education. House and Senate committees responsible for education legislation were more liberal than the House or Senate as a whole, therefore more receptive to equal educational opportunity and to active federal support of bilingual-bicultural programs.

The division of a Republican president and a Democratic Congress significantly affected the final legislation. The administration itself was divided over the value of bilingual-bicultural education and the appropriate federal role.

The Supreme Court decision of *Lau* v. *Nichols*, while merely supporting the Senate determination to produce an expansion of bilingual-bicultural education, substantially influenced the House and administration positions. Public opinion had minimal influence on the legislative outcome.

Federal support for bilingual-bicultural education related to congressional acceptance of the goal of equal educational opportunity. Federal support for bilingual-bicultural education also rested in part on its similarity to federal compensatory-education programs.

Neither revolutionary nor reactionary, the 1974 Bilingual Education Act represented a reform of existing law and practice in bilingual-bicultural education. It emphasized the bilingual-bicultural aspects of federal programs, authorized funds for personnel preparation and for curricula development, and extended the bilingual-bicultural approach to adult and vocational education. The law also gave greater priority to the bilingual program within the Office of Education.

Acknowledgements

Full acknowledgement needs to be given to those who have provided valuable assistance in the preparation of this dissertation. My deepest appreciation is extended to the three members of the University of Maryland research committee: Dr. Janet R. Baird, an inspiring teacher and friend who directed the dissertation; Dr. Jean D. Grambs and Dr. William E. DeLorenzo, who shared their knowledge, extended constant support, and offered valuable advice. I also thank Dr. George Male of the University of Maryland and Dr. Rudolph Troike, director of the Center of Applied Linguistics and a noted scholar in the field of bilingual-bicultural education, for serving on the committee.

I am grateful to the staff of the Congressional Reading Room in the Library of Congress, particularly Margaret Whitlock and Winston Tabb, Jim Blakely and Harvey Baugh III, for their research assistance.

This dissertation could not have been written without the extraordinary access to primary materials permitted by congressional staff, administration officials, and lobbying group leaders. Rarely is a researcher permitted to interview political leaders and have access to the files of their staff while those individuals are still in public life. For that reason, I particularly owe a debt to Senators Edward M. Kennedy and Alan Cranston and to Representatives Herman Badillo, Alphonzo Bell, Albert Quie, and William Steiger. Those Senate staff members who were of special help in giving me guidance, time, and documents were Mark Schneider, Gary Aldrich, Jonathan Steinberg, and Doris Ullman. Those House staff members who went out of their way to aid my efforts were Shirley Downs, Christopher Cross, Jack Jennings, Sharon Holroyd, and Janet Kuhn. Particularly helpful in obtaining administration materials were Charles Cooke and Kathy Truex. Lobbyists who were generous in providing information were Manuel Fierro, Pepe Barrón, Greg Humphries, Linda Chávez, and Charles Lee.

A special note of appreciation goes to Helmi Cotter for her superior typing skills, her excellent editing, and her long hours of extra work in preparing this manuscript. Also deserving thanks are Margie Holman, Thelma Rubinstein, and John Cotter for their assistance in the preparation of portions of the manuscript. My mother, Roslyn Gilbert, deserves a special mention, not only for her general support but for her typing of portions of the manuscript draft.

My deepest gratitude to my husband, Mark, and my son, Aaron, who shared fully in the experience of this dissertation. Mark offered special "midnight editing" and his own expertise, which helped to guide my efforts.

I also wish to thank my friends and my neighbors, Jean and Michael Levin, for their support and encouragement.

Finally, I would like to dedicate this dissertation to the memory of my father, Mitchell Goldberg-Gilbert, and to my father-in-law, Benjamin Schneider, who as first-generation Americans struggled to assimilate yet retain their rich cultural heritage.

Table of Contents

INTRODUCTION

The Scope of the Dissertation

On 21 August, the Education Amendments of 1974 were signed into law. The law extended and amended the Elementary and Secondary Education Act of 1965. Section 105, dealing with bilingual-bicultural education, was the first major amendment to Title VII since the enactment of the Bilingual Education Act of 1968.

This dissertation is an exploration of the development of the 1974 Bilingual Education Act and the differing philosophies which are melded by that act into the current view of bilingual-bicultural education. The dissertation asks whether this 1974 law represents a reaction against the experience of the past, a reform of the federal program, or a revolutionary change in the character of the federal view of bilingual-bicultural education.

The increase in federal attention to bilingual-bicultural education has paralleled an increased concern of educators, legislators, and jurists with the responsibility of the American public school system for ensuring equality of educational opportunity. The public school system has been conceived of as an equalizing factor in American society.[1] It is the medium by which generations of immigrants are integrated into a new culture and society. During the 1960s and 1970s linguistic-minority groups have begun asserting new demands for the educational institutions to recognize and respond to their differences, demands which the legal institutions to some degree have supported.

As a nation pledged to educational equality, the contrast between the numbers of limited-English-speaking children who need special language programs and the limited number of educational programs designed to fulfill that need raises fundamental questions of social equality. Therefore, it is important to understand the direction chartered by the 1974 act. Is it a reaction against the rising pressures of numerically small minority groups? Is it a modest reform and an improvement of an existing trend of increased federal concern? Or is it a revolution that marks a sharp break with our past educational practice?

In order to answer these questions, the dissertation includes the following areas. Chapter 1 presents the scope of the dissertation, a definition of terms, a review of the limitations of the study, the sources of data, and the purpose of the dissertation.

Chapter 2 describes the need for bilingual-bicultural programs, the history of linguistic minorities in the United States, and the response of public schools to those groups, including the major approaches now used for teaching those minorities. The chapter also reviews the literature in the field of bilingual-bicultural education, particularly as it relates to federal involvement.

Chapter 3 examines the legislative history and the philosophy and breadth of federal bilingual-bicultural education legislation through 1973.

Chapters 4, 5, and 6, respectively, describe the development of the Senate, House, and administration positions on the key issues pertaining to the 1974 act. The roles of key legislators, staff aides, lobbyists, administration officials, and court decisions are noted.

Chapter 7 examines the resolution of issues in the conference between the House and Senate on the 1974 act and examines presidential action on the law. The chapter also outlines the changes contained in the 1974 law and the results of passage.

Chapter 8 presents a summary and analysis of the 1974 act and lists the research questions and findings. The chapter analyzes the implications of the changes contained within the 1974 act to demonstrate whether they represent a revolution, a reaction, or a reform of the federal role in bilingual-bicultural education legislation. Finally, implications for future research are noted.

Bilingual-Bicultural Education Defined

To facilitate the discussion of the legislative history, a basic requirement is an understanding of the standard definition of bilingual-bicultural education. Since the initial proposal of federal legislation in 1967, bilingual-bicultural education has become an increasingly emotion-charged issue. Much of the controversy has stemmed from definitional ambiguity and disagreement over goals. The term "bilingual education" is found generally in the literature prior to 1973. After 1973, however, the term "bilingual-bicultural education" is used more frequently. For the purposes of this dissertation, the term "bilingual-bicultural education" is used.

Bilingual education is explicitly defined in the Project Manual accompanying Title VII of the Elementary and Secondary Education Amendments (ESEA). The Project Manual of the Office of Education, which established guidelines for the implementation of bilingual programs, states: "bilingual-education is the use of two languages, one of which is English, as mediums of instruction for the same pupil population in a well-organized program. . . . "[2]

A distinction between "bilingual education" and "bilingual-bicultural education" is made by the U.S. Commission on Civil Rights. The director of the U.S. Commission on Civil Rights declared:

. . . Bilingual-bicultural education is an instructional program in which two languages—English and the native tongue—are used as mediums of instruction and in which the cultural background of the students is incorporated into the curriculum. This is distinguished from a program, which may be bilingual, but which fails to incorporate the cultural backgrounds of students and, thus, cannot be considered bicultural.[3]

Bilingual-bicultural education is defined in another source as:

A process which uses a pupil's primary language as the principal source of instruction while at the same time systematically and sequentially teaching him the language of the predominant culture. This teaching process will provide a cultural environment within which pupils can foster their cultural heritage as well as enrich their cognitive and verbal processes. The purpose of such a bicultural environment is to make the pupil bilingual through conceptualizing in the language best known to him, and by this approach to become a bilingual-bicultural citizen.[4]

It was the discussion preceding the 1967 law which focussed attention on the necessity and the federal responsibility to meet the needs of limited-English speakers within the schools. In its declaration of policy, Title VII states:

In recognition of the special educational needs of the large numbers of children of limited English-speaking ability in the United States, Congress hereby declares it to be the policy of the United States to provide financial assistance to local educational agencies to develop and carry out new and imaginative elementary and secondary school programs designed to meet these special educational needs.[5]

Note must be made of the difference between a "limited English-speaking" and a "non-English-speaking" child. Children of limited English-speaking ability are defined as "children who speak a language other than English in their home environment and who are less capable of performing school work in English than in the primary language."[6] A non-English-speaking child is defined as "a child who communicates in his or her home language only. Such a child is unable to conduct basic conversations in English or take advantage of classroom instruction in English."[7]

Limitations of the Dissertation

This dissertation examines the legislative history of the 1974 Bilingual Education Amendments with a review of pertinent prior federal legislation. It does not evaluate current federally funded bilingual-bicultural programs nor does it review bilingual-bicultural programs at the state or community level. It does not examine the political controversy and conflicting opinions relating to bilingual-bicultural education which exist among different linguistic and ethnic groups. It does not evaluate current studies of alternative classroom methodology used in bilingual-bicultural education. It does not analyze the effects of positions on bilingual-bicultural education on congressional candidates or on electoral outcomes. Not all participants responded to interview requests; therefore, interviews are limited to those who agreed to participate. The review of literature is limited to those works completed since 1962, with emphasis on the current literature to 1975.

Sources of Data and Information

This dissertation reviews the literature in the field of bilingual-bicultural education as it relates to the legislation. It also relies directly on administration studies, reports and memoranda, congressional hearings, and congressional committee reports and memoranda, as well as pertinent court decisions. Key and available congressional leaders and staff, administration officials and staff, and lobbyists and educators who played a leading role in the 1974 law are interviewed. The letters requesting interviews and the interview forms are shown in Appendixes K through P. The importance of other legislative history models is noted.

The Purpose of the Dissertation

A legislative history of the bilingual-bicultural provisions of the Education Amendments of 1974, Public Law 93-380, and an understanding of the implications of the new statute are essential in analyzing how this nation is coping with a major educational challenge—the education of five million limited English-speaking children.[8] This legislative history documents the differing views, including contrasting educational philosophies concerning the teaching of limited English-speaking children, as they are presented by senators, congressmen, interest groups, and the respective federal agencies. In so doing, this dissertation traces the formation of the consensus represented by the bilingual-bicultural provisions of Public Law 93-380. That consensus already has altered significantly the federal role in bilingual-bicultural education. It is likely to continue doing so in the future. At the same time, the legislative history of the bilingual-bicultural provisions illuminates the recesses of the legislative process where ideals, traditions, private interests, personalities, and partisan politics interacted to produce this public law containing a new public policy toward bilingual-bicultural education.

In addition, an understanding of legislative history can help others who seek to explore new legislative areas—the problems to be faced and the strategies needed to cope with and solve these problems. An examination of prior legislative histories shows that the fundamental technique used is the case study. Case studies focus on one policy issue or governmental action and provide the basis for generalizations about the political process.[9] Marmor's legislative history of Medicare shows that a case study aids in the analysis and interpretation of the policy-making process.[10] Bailey's legislative history of the Employment Act of 1946 presents a picture of the formulation of a public policy in Congress from its inception to passage into law.[11]

INTERVIEW NOTES

Joshua Fishman, Institute for Advanced Studies, Princeton University, New Jersey.

NOTES

[1]Horace Mann, "Twelfth Annual Report on Education (1848)," in *Theory and Practice in the History of American Education*, ed. James W. Hillesheim and George D. Merrill (Pacific Palisades, California: Goodyear Publishing Company, 1971), p. 154.

[2]U.S., Department of Health, Education, and Welfare, Office of Education, *Manual for Project Applicants and Grantees: Programs under Bilingual Education Act, Title VII, ESEA-Draft, March 30, 1970*, p. 1.

[3]U.S., Congress, Senate Committee on Labor and Public Welfare, Education Legislation of 1973, *Hearings before a Subcommittee on Education of the Senate Committee on Labor and Public Welfare on S. 1539*, 93rd Cong., 1st sess., 1973, p. 2600.

[4]State Department of Education, California Bilingual-Bicultural Task Force, "Master Plan for Bilingual-Bicultural Education," Sacramento, California, 17 July 1972, p. 2. (Mimeographed.)

[5]*Elementary and Secondary Education Act, Statutes at Large* 81, sec. 702, 806 (1968).

[6]Hannah N. Geffert et al., *The Current Status of U.S. Bilingual Education Legislation*, Bilingual Education Series, no. 4 (Arlington, Virginia: Center for Applied Linguistics, May 1975), p. 44.

[7]Ibid.

[8]Interview with Joshua Fishman, Institute for Advanced Studies, Princeton University, New Jersey.

[9]Theodore R. Marmor, *The Politics of Medicare* (Chicago, Illinois: Aldine Publishing Company, 1970), p. v.

[10]Ibid., p. vii.

[11]Stephen Bailey, *Congress Makes a Law: The Story behind the Employment Act of 1946* (New York: Columbia University Press, 1950), p. ix.

Memory Organization, Bilingualism, and Interlingual Interference: A Comparative Analysis of the Semantic Distance and Semantic Judgment of English Monolingual and Spanish-English Bilingual Students

Ramanand Durga

Second Place, Outstanding Dissertations
National Advisory Council on Bilingual Education

Degree conferred February 1978
Fordham University
New York, New York

Dissertation Committee:
Claire Ashby-Davis, *Chair*
Trina Lawson
Carolyn Hedley
Richard Baecher

The original version of this article appeared under the title, "Bilingualism and Interlingual Interference," by Ramanand Durga, published in *JOURNAL OF CROSS-CULTURAL PSYCHOLOGY*, Vol. 9, No. 4 (Dec. 1978), pp. 401-415, and is reprinted herewith by permission of the publisher, Sage Publications, Inc.

About the Author

Dr. Ramanand Durga is the Associate Director of the Educational Improvement Center-Northeast, an arm of the New Jersey State Department of Education. Dr. Durga's main interest is in the area of cognitive development and interlingual interference among bilingual children. His experience includes working as a bilingual teacher for several years in the New York City public school system and as an assistant professor of bilingual education at the Graduate School of Education at Rutgers University.

ABSTRACT

The hypothesis of interlingual interference was tested by employing the network model of the semantic memory. Ninety-three true-false propositions were presented to English monolinguals and Spanish-English bilingual subjects. Two variables were measured: the reaction time to the true-false items and the semantic judgment. It was found that subjects operating in a monolingual context performed equally well. However, the performance of subjects operating in a dual-language context was significantly impaired. Difference in hierarchical organization of the semantic memory for the two languages was an important factor in determining interlingual interference.

STATEMENT OF THE PROBLEM

In the field of bilingual education, scholars are divided upon the issue of linguistic interference. Those who argue against interference maintain that the two languages of bilinguals are independent of each other (Macnamara 1967; Tulving and Colotla 1970). They contend that bilinguals form stronger associations among words within each of their languages than across the two languages. Thus, the possibility of interlingual interference is reduced to a minimum and is most likely not greater than intralingual interference. Some studies supporting the language-independence hypothesis even went further to demonstrate that when items are presented to bilingual subjects in one language, the recall effect of the items is the same as when they are presented in the bilinguals' second language (Kolers 1966; Tulving and Colotla 1970; Glanzer and Duarte 1971). According to Tulving and Colotla, this effect is probably due to a well-established habit of translating from one language to another.

Both positions described above (language independence and translation-equivalence effect) have been under severe attack by scholars investigating interlingual interference among bilingual subjects (Dalrymple-Alford 1968; Kintsch and Kintsch 1968; Dalrymple-Alford and Aamiry 1970; López and Young 1974). However, these studies yielded highly contradictory findings about interlingual interference. Dalrymple-Alford, and Dalrymple-Alford and Aamiry refuted the idea of linguistic independence while supporting the hypothesis of a translation-equivalence effect. Young and Navar, Kintsch and Kintsch, and López and Young questioned the language-independence and translation-equivalence hypotheses while Macnamara (1967) and Tulving and Colotla (1970) provided data in support of both hypotheses.

The contradictory results yielded by these studies may be due to the nature of the experimental tasks involved (Kintsch and Kintsch

1969). Besides, such tasks were designed according to the paired-associate paradigm or a variation of it. The paired-associate paradigm is inadequate to probe interference across languages (López and Young 1974) since the same relative difficulty of list-words may not be obtained when translated into another language. It was the purpose of this study to investigate linguistic interference among Spanish-English bilingual subjects by employing the network model of the semantic memory.

According to Collins and Quillian (1969), there are two possible organizations of verbal information in the memory. First, people may store each word (node) with its set of attributes and retrieve each separately for utilization, a process known as *successive scanning*. Secondly, there may be an alternative organization in the form of a more generalized interrelationship between sets of nodes. Retrieval of verbal information in this case would then follow a logical and systematic manner based upon the interconnection of the nodes, a process known as *category access*. The network model evolves from the second organization of linguistic information in the semantic memory, and it depicts a huge network of concepts and the patterns of their interrelationship. The concepts, according to the model, are hierarchically organized into logically nested subordinate and superordinate relations. A property that is characteristic of a particular class of things is assumed to be stored only at the location in the hierarchy that corresponds to that class.

For instance, in Rumelhart et al. (1972), *robin* and *bird* exist as two separate nodes in the proposition *A robin is a bird*, connected by the *is a* relation. Besides, attributes such as *fly* and *wings* are stored with the node *birds*. To verify the proposition *A robin can fly*, an individual may enter the memory store where *birds* is found and logically deduce that *robin* is a *bird* and birds can fly. Therefore, a robin can fly. It will also take the individual longer to verify the proposition *A robin is an animal* than to verify *A robin is a bird*, since she/he has to go from *robin* to its superordinate, *bird*, and, finally, to *animal*.

The key terms used in this study may now be defined. For the purpose of the present investigation, the definition of semantic distance offered by Rips et al. (1973) was used. They defined the term as the memorial representations of the underlying semantic structure that links a subset with its superset. For example, the memorial representations for *canary* and *bird* would be more closely related than those for *canary* and *animal*. Semantic judgment is defined as the estimation of the meaning of a particular lexical item after processing the complete semantic network of that item. Finally, reaction time is the time that elapses between the exposure of a proposition and the subject's response.

Within the conceptual framework of the network model described above, the following three hypotheses were posed:

Hypothesis 1. Verbal information in the semantic memory is stored in a similar hierarchy of categories in both English and Spanish. This hypothesis will be supported if there is no significant difference in semantic distance between the English monolingual and the Spanish-dominant bilingual subjects on the same stimulus items presented in the two languages.

Hypothesis 2. Nodes in the hierarchical structure of the semantic memory in one language may not have a corresponding equivalent in the other language. This hypothesis will be supported if there is a significant difference in semantic judgment between the English monolinguals and the Spanish-dominant bilingual subjects.

Hypothesis 3. If there is a significant difference in semantic judgment between the English monolinguals and the Spanish-dominant bilinguals, then the semantic distance of the apparent bilingual subjects operating in a dual-language context will be significantly greater than that of either the English monolinguals or the Spanish-dominant bilingual subjects. This hypothesis is based upon the assumption that one linguistic system of the apparent bilinguals will intrude upon the other (linguistic interference) when processing linguistic items interpolated in the two languages.

METHOD

Subjects

The subjects consisted of forty students (twenty male and twenty female) drawn from the ninth grade of a senior high school in the following manner. Ten subjects of Anglo-American descent (five male and five female) were drawn randomly from the English-speaking monolingual population. The remaining thirty subjects, all of whom were of Hispanic descent, were drawn from the bilingual population so that there were twenty students (ten male and ten female) who were equally competent in both languages (apparent bilinguals) and ten students (five male and five female) who were dominant in the Spanish language. Each bilingual was matched to one monolingual subject on reading score, age, sex, and socioeconomic status. As a result of the matching process, the apparent bilinguals were divided into two subgroups, A and B.

Materials

The *Home Bilingual Usage Estimate* (Skozcylas 1971), the *Hollingshead Index* (Hollingshead and Redlich 1967), and the *Test of Reading—Inter-American Series* (Guidance Testing Associates 1967) were used to collect data to match the subjects. To measure the dependent variables, the researcher designed and validated the *Test of Semantic Distance* and the *Test of Semantic Judgment*. Three stopwatches capable of measuring reaction time to the nearest hundredth of a second and four cassette tape recorders to tape students' responses were also used.

The *Test of Semantic Distance* consisted of ninety-three true-false items (forty-eight true statements and forty-five false ones), all of which were in the form of "An S is a P." The predicate nouns were chosen from the following sub- and superordinate categories: dish, inanimate object, fruit, food, bird, and animal. The subject noun was an instance of these categories. In choosing the instances from each category, the investigator employed the procedure used by Henley (1969) and Rips et al. (1973).

Thirty-nine freshmen students from a Catholic high school were asked to list as many instances as possible from each category within a seven-minute period. The first seventeen most frequently listed items from each category were then checked against the Thorndike-Lorge (1944) semantic word list for their frequency of usage in English. All the items chosen were among the first six thousand most frequently used words in English. The word count for each item was above fifty at the seventh-grade level. Their translation equivalents into Spanish were then checked against Eaton's semantic word list (1961) to equate for frequency of usage in Spanish. The ordering of the sentences is based upon the method used by Rips et al. (1973) and is illustrated in table 1.

There were two language versions of the *Test of Semantic Distance* and two alternate forms: an English version, a Spanish version, and two forms of an English-Spanish version. The test items in the two forms were randomly either in English or Spanish. Those items which appeared in English in one form reappeared in Spanish in the other, but in a different sequence. A test-retest reliability of .93 was found. Construct validity was obtained by having three psychologists rate each item on a ten-point scale.

The *Test of Semantic Judgment* consisted of the same lexical items which were used in the *Test of Semantic Distance*, but the procedure in designing the test differed. Each lexical item appeared as a standard word followed by four comparison words. Three comparison words were subcategories of the standard word and the fourth

Table 1
Ordering of the True-False Sentences

TRUE SENTENCES		
LEVEL I (24)		
An *Sd* is a dish. (8)	An *Sb* is a bird. (8)	An *Sf* is a fruit. (8)
LEVEL II (24)		
An *Sd* is an inanimate object. (8)	An *Sb* is an animal. (8)	An *Sf* is a food. (8)

FALSE SENTENCES		
An *Sd* is a fruit. (5)	An *Sb* is a fruit. (5)	An *Sf* is a dish. (5)
An *Sd* is a food. (5)	An *Sb* is a dish. (5)	An *Sf* is a bird. (5)
An *Sd* is a bird. (5)	An *Sb* is an inanimate object. (5)	An *Sf* is an animal. (5)

was an unrelated subcategory. The subjects were asked to indicate the degree of relatedness between the standard word and each of the comparison words on a four-point scale. The test was prepared in two language versions (English and Spanish). It yielded a test-retest reliability of .87 over a two-week interval. A construct validity of .91 was obtained by having three psychologists sort each of the comparison words according to the degree of relatedness to the standard word. The percentage of answers that the three psychologists agreed upon was used as an index of validity.

Procedures

Information on the subjects' age and sex were obtained from the students' cumulative records, while the two-factor *Hollingshead Index* was used to ascertain socioeconomic status. To obtain the reading score, the English version of the *Test of Reading—Inter-American Series* was administered to the English monolinguals, and the English and Spanish versions were both administered to the bilingual sample five weeks apart. The *Home Bilingual Usage Estimate* was also administered to the bilingual sample to determine the degree of bilingualism of each Spanish-speaking subject. According to this test, the bilingual subjects were classified either as apparent bilinguals or Spanish-dominant bilinguals. Marginal cases were eliminated. The data collected thus far were used to match the bilingual subjects with the English monolinguals.

Prior to measuring the dependent variables, three graduate bilingual examiners of Hispanic descent and one research specialist of Anglo-American descent were trained to administer the *Test of Semantic Distance* individually. Using subjects other than those participating in the experiment, the examiners were given the opportunity to demonstrate their proficiency to criterion level. Intra- and inter-examiner reliability was determined by having the examiners unknowingly administer selected test items to the same subject twice and by comparing the scores for each examiner. Intra-examiner reliability was found to be .92 and inter-examiner reliability was determined to be .89.

Preceding the actual testing, each subject was told that a statement would be presented to him and that he was required to verify the statement as true or false as quickly as he could, but as accurately as possible. He was then given ten practice trials in the appropriate language. The predicate nouns in the statements for practice trials were taken from categories other than those used in the actual test. In the case of the apparent bilinguals, an even number of practice trials was given in both languages, but in random sequence. To ensure that the apparent bilinguals attended to the language as well as the meaning conveyed in the statements, they were instructed that a response could only be considered correct if it occurred in the same language in which the stimulus item was presented.

Each true-false statement was typed in bold letters (IBM Orator) in the center of a white 8 × 5-inch card, all of which were bound by two rings so that one card could be flipped over at a time to expose one statement. The stopwatch was started simultaneously by the examiner. Each stimulus item was exposed for three seconds. The subject's response terminated the sentence presentation, and the watch was stopped. There was an interval of about ten seconds between the presentation of each stimulus. The English version of the *Test of Semantic Distance* was given to the English monolinguals and the Spanish version was administered to the Spanish-dominant bilinguals. Group A of the apparent bilinguals received one of the two alternate forms of the English-Spanish version while Group B received the other. Immediately upon completion of the *Test of Semantic Distance*, the English monolingual and Spanish-dominant bilingual subjects were sent across to an adjacent room to take the *Test of Semantic Judgment*, administered collectively in the appropriate language.

RESULTS

To assess the semantic distance for each group, the reaction time for level one of each true statement was subtracted from that of level two. To ascertain the directionality of the resultant semantic distance, the *Wilcoxon Matched-Pairs Signed-Rank Test* was employed. An algebraic sign (+ for positive numbers and – for negative numbers) was assigned to each T-unit. The sign that occurred the least was summed to obtain a value for T. The magnitude of the differences between each group was computed by ranking the difference between level one and two for each lexical item. Examination of the direction revealed that there was an increase in reaction time as the classification categories for the subject nouns become more encompassing or inclusive, $T (24) = 3, p < .01$.

The multiple-classification analysis of variance with repeated measures for matched groups was employed to analyze the semantic distance across groups. The results revealed significant difference between groups, $F (3, 38) = 15.96, p < .01$. To pursue the difference revealed by the analysis further, the *t*-test was employed. When the mean semantic distance of the English monolinguals was compared with that for the Spanish-dominant bilinguals, no significant difference was found, $t (19) = 1.48, p > .05$. Thus, the first hypothesis was confirmed.

The semantic-judgment data for both the English monolingual and the Spanish-dominant bilingual subjects were analyzed with the *t*-test. A comparison of the mean score between the two ethnic groups revealed a significant difference in semantic judgment, $t (19) = 2.39$, $p < .025$, which confirmed the second hypothesis.

An item analysis of the linguistic category *dish*, on the *Test of Semantic Distance*, substantiated the findings of the *Test of Semantic Judgment*. When the Spanish-dominant bilinguals were asked to verify the proposition *La taza es un plato*, nine out of ten subjects responded that it was false. This trend of response was evident in all but two of the items of this linguistic category. The two exceptions were *El plato es un plato* and *El platillo es un plato*. In these two cases, the subject nouns were identical to the predicate nouns since the word *plato* has double meanings in Spanish (*plate* and *dish*) and *platillo* is the diminutive of *plato*.

Further item analysis also revealed a difference in hierarchical structure in the semantic memory between the two languages for the linguistic category *birds*. In Spanish, two parallel linguistic categories exist for the English subcategory *bird*. *Chicken* and *duck* were not considered *birds* in Spanish by the Spanish-dominant bilinguals. The two lexical items were considered under a separate subcategory called *ave*, which corresponds in English to *domesticated birds*, as opposed to *pájaro*, which refers to *undomesticated birds* such as robin and canary.

The data analyzed so far provide evidence in support of the first two hypotheses. Analysis of the data for the third hypothesis is contingent upon the evidence already provided. It was found that verbal information in the semantic memory is stored in a hierarchy of categories in both English and Spanish. Besides, some nodes in the hierarchical structure of one language do not have corresponding equivalents in the other. Because of the absence of corresponding equivalents in the two languages, it is expected that the apparent bilingual subjects will take significantly more time to process verbal information and to arrive at a semantic judgment when operating in a dual-language context.

Analysis of the mean semantic distance of the English monolinguals when compared with that for the apparent bilinguals in Group A yielded a significant difference, $t(19) = 3.28. p < .01$. There was also a significant difference in semantic distance when the English monolinguals were compared with the apparent bilinguals in Group B, $t(19) = 4.09. p < .01$. The differences, in both cases, were in favor of the English monolinguals, who took significantly less time to process verbal information in order to arrive at a semantic judgment.

Examination of the mean semantic distance of the Spanish-dominant bilingual subjects and both groups of the apparent bilinguals yielded significant differences in favor of the Spanish-dominant bilinguals, $t(19) = 2.90, p < .01$; and $t(19) = 4.29, p < .01$. The semantic distance of the apparent bilingual subjects who were operating in a dual-language context was therefore significantly greater than that of either the English monolingual or the Spanish-dominant bilingual subject.

To substantiate that the greater semantic distance of the apparent bilinguals was a result of the intrusion of one linguistic system upon the other, the subjects' responses on the cassette tapes were analyzed. The analysis revealed that when the propositions were presented in Spanish and followed by a proposition in English, seven out of eight times there was a complete or incomplete semantic judgment based upon the Spanish category structure for the English propositions. The reverse was also true when the English propositions presented were followed by Spanish propositions. The complete or incomplete semantic judgment was then followed by the correct one in the appropriate language, hence the greater semantic distance of the apparent bilinguals.

CONCLUSIONS

The findings of this study indicated that verbal information in the semantic memory is stored in a hierarchical organization for both languages (English and Spanish). The results support that of Collins and Quillian (1969) who argued that the more remote a superordinate is from the subject of a sentence, the longer it will take the subject to retrieve the necessary information to verify the truth or falsity of the sentence. However, this finding cannot be generalized beyond the linguistic items chosen for the study since other studies (Rips et al. 1973; Smith et al. 1974) have indicated that this factor might not be true for all linguistic categories. The extent to which this is true depends upon the frequency of usage of the linguistic items in the language (Smith et al. 1974). The items selected for the present study were based upon their frequency of usage in both languages.

Examination of the semantic-judgment data for the English monolinguals and the Spanish-dominant bilingual subjects revealed significant difference between the two ethnic groups. In other words, nodes in the hierarchical structure of the semantic memory in one language did not have corresponding equivalents in the other. Figures 1 and 2 depict the hierarchical structure of the semantic memory for a typical English monolingual subject and a typical Spanish-domi-

Figure 1
Structure of the Semantic Memory of a Typical Spanish-English Bilingual for Linguistic Category A

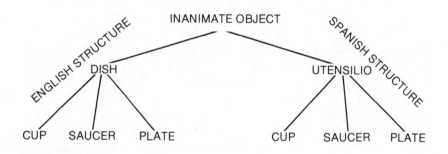

Figure 2
Structure of the Semantic Memory of a Typical Spanish-English Bilingual for Linguistic Category B

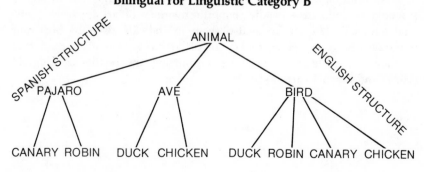

nant bilingual subject for the two linguistic categories *dishes* and *birds*. Analysis of the semantic-judgment data for linguistic category A revealed that there was no Spanish equivalent for the English subcategory *dish*. On the other hand, when linguistic category B was considered, there were two different nodes in Spanish for the English subcategory *bird*. For the third linguistic category *fruit*, it seems that the English nodes had corresponding equivalents in Spanish.

As identified in the study, the differences in category structure across the two languages were of two kinds: the vertical difference and the horizontal difference. Vertical difference in category structure means that a subcategory in one language does not correspond to the same subcategory in the other language. For instance, *dish*, in English, had no corresponding subcategory in Spanish and was subsumed under *utensilio*. In other words, vertical difference occurred between subcategory and superordinate category structures (figure 1). Horizontal difference occurred within a particular subcategory. For example, linguistic items which are subsumed under the English subcategory *birds* are subsumed under two separate but parallel subcategories in Spanish, *ave* and *pájaro*. An important distinguishing factor between the two kinds of semantic structures is that vertical difference will result in a difference of semantic distance as well as semantic judgment, but horizontal difference will only yield a difference in semantic judgment.

The findings of this study revealed significant differences in semantic distance between the apparent bilingual and the English monolingual subjects. There was also significant difference in semantic distance between the apparent bilingual and the Spanish-dominant bilingual subjects. In both cases the apparent bilinguals took significantly more time to process verbal information interpolated in the two languages. An analysis of the subjects' responses on the cassette tapes indicated that the longer time taken by the apparent bilinguals to process verbal information interpolated in the two languages was due to an intrusion of one linguistic system upon the other. (Unlike the semantic memory of the English monolinguals or that of the Spanish-dominant bilingual subjects, the complete diagram in figure 1 would be indicative of the semantic memory of an apparent bilingual subject). The findings also seem to indicate that the apparent bilinguals have a greater repertoire of verbal information than that of their monolingual peers, thus supporting the results of Leopold (1971) and Ianco-Worrall (1972).

REFERENCES

Collins, A.M., and Quillian, M.R. "Retrieval Time from Semantic Memory." *Journal of Verbal Learning and Verbal Behavior* 8 (April 1969): 240-47.

Dalrymple-Alford, E. "Inter-lingual Interference in a Color-Naming Task." *Psychonomic Science* 10, 25 February 1969, pp. 215-16.

_____, and Aamiry, A. "Word Associations of Bilinguals." *Psychonomic Science* 21, 25 December 1970, pp. 319-20.

Eaton, H.S. *An English-French-German-Spanish Word Frequency Dictionary.* New York: Dover Publications, 1961.

Glanzer, M., and Duarte, A. "Repetition Between and Within Languages in Free Recall." *Journal of Verbal Learning and Verbal Behavior* 10 (December 1971): 625-30.

Guidance Testing Associates. Manual-Tests of General Ability and Tests of Reading—Inter-American Series Forms CE, DE, CEs, DEs. Austin, Texas, 1967. (Address: 6516 Shirley Avenue, Austin, Texas 78752.)

Henley, N.M. "A Psychological Study of the Semantics of Animal Terms." *Journal of Verbal Learning and Verbal Behavior* 8 (April 1969): 176-84.

Hollingshead, A.B., and Redlich, F.C. *Social Class and Mental Illness.* New York: John Wiley, 1967.

Ianco-Worrall, A. "Bilingualism and Cognitive Development." *Child Development* 43 (December 1972): 1390-1400.

Kintsch, W., and Kintsch, E. "Interlingual Interference and Memory Process." *Journal of Verbal Learning and Verbal Behavior* 8 (February 1969): 16-19.

Kolers, P. "Reading and Talking Bilingually." *American Journal of Psychology* 79 (September 1966): 357-76.

_____. "Translation and Bilingualism." In *Communication, Language, and Meaning,* edited by G. Miller, pp. 280-90. New York: Basic Books, 1973.

Leopold, W.F. "The Study of Child Language and Infant Bilingualism." In *Child Language,* edited by A. Bar-Adon and W.F. Leopold, pp. 1-13. Englewood Cliffs, N.J.: Prentice-Hall, 1971.

López, M., and Young, R. "The Linguistic Interdependence of Bilinguals." *Journal of Experimental Psychology* 102 (June 1974): 981-83.

Macnamara, J. "The Linguistic Independence of Bilinguals." *Journal of Verbal Learning and Verbal Behavior* 6 (October 1967): 729-36.

Rips, L. J.; Shoben, E. J.; and Smith, E. E. "Semantic Distance and the Verification of Semantic Relations." *Journal of Verbal Learning and Verbal Behavior* 12 (February 1973): 1-20.

Rumelhart, D.E.; Lindsay, P.H.; and Norman, D.A. "A Process Model for Long-Term Memory." In *Organization of Memory*, edited by E. Tulving and W. Donaldson, pp. 198-246. New York: Academic Press, 1972.

Skozcylas, R. *Home Bilingual Usage Estimate*. Gilroy, California: R.V. Skozcylas, 1971.

Smith, E.E.; Shoben, E.J.; and Rips, L.J. "Structure and Process in Semantic Memory: Featural Model for Semantic Decisions." *Psychological Review* 81 (May 1974): 214-41.

Thorndike, E.L., and Lorge, I. *The Teacher's Word Book of 30,000 Words*. New York: Columbia University Press, 1944.

Tulving, E., and Colotla, V.A. "Free Recall in Trilingual Lists." *Cognitive Psychology* 1 (January 1970): 86-98.

Young, R.K., and Navar, I. "Retroactive Inhibition with Bilinguals." *Journal of Experimental Psychology* 77 (May 1968): 109-15.

The Effect of Auditory Discrimination Training of Spanish-Speaking Children on Auditory Discrimination and Sound-Letter Associations

Virginia Reyes Kramer

Third Place, Outstanding Dissertations
National Advisory Council on Bilingual Education

Degree conferred May 1978
Kansas State University
Manhattan, Kansas

Dissertation Committee:
Leo M. Schell, *Chair*
James Armagost
James Boyer
Robert Newhouse

About the Author

Dr. Virginia Reyes Kramer is currently self-employed as a consultant in bilingual education and as a Spanish translator for the Cooperative Extension Service at Kansas State University. She also serves as the president of the Kansas Association for Bilingual Education and the scholarship fund raiser/project coordinator for the KSU Mexican American Alumni Association. Her experience includes positions as a high school Spanish teacher and as an administrative assistant in a program designed to prepare students to teach in inner city schools with large concentrations of Spanish-speaking children.

ABSTRACT

The study had two purposes. One was to investigate whether or not a four-week ear-training program would help bilingual Spanish-speaking children score better on an auditory-discrimination test than similar children without such training. The other was to investigate whether the ear-training program would help Spanish-speaking children make sound-letter associations more easily in a follow-up phonics program. The results showed that the ear-training program was effective in helping Spanish-speaking children more easily discriminate English sounds identified as difficult for them. This was true both for sounds taught and sounds not taught. Analysis of the phonics tests showed there was no significant difference between groups on either of the two phonics posttests or the retention tests. This indicated that the auditory-discrimination training program had no effect on the experimental subjects' abilities to learn phonics. However, the mean scores for the phonics-word pretest gave evidence that the improved sound-discrimination skills did help the experimental subjects in word analysis.

THEORETICAL FRAMEWORK

Reading is a language-based activity. It is the children's syntactic and phonological command of language plus past environmental and cultural experiences that give schools a base with which to begin teaching reading skills. When children begin reading at around age six, they have mastered most of the sound system of their language (Gibson and Levin 1975; Harris and Smith 1976; Shuy 1970). At this same age, it has been suggested that there is little in the grammar or syntax of language that an average child does not know (Dechant 1970). Also, a strong base for learning to read has been established by age six because of environmental and cultural experiences which will make it easier for young readers to predict meaning (Harris and Smith 1976). Therefore, it is the reader's knowledge of the various components of language and experiential background that helps the child to interpret graphic symbols into meaningful units.

In recent years, one language component, auditory discrimination, has been evaluated more closely with respect to its role in the reading process. Auditory discrimination is the ability to discriminate the sound parts or phonemes of words (Robeck and Wilson 1974). In order to read successfully, children need to be able to associate the sounds in spoken words with their corresponding graphemes. Before this can happen, Gibson and Levin (1975) have noted that fragmentation and recombination of sounds are prerequisites to mastering speech and for decoding it into written symbols. Savin (1972) has stated that learning to read is not simply a matter of phoneme-grapheme association. According to Savin, beginning readers first must be able to perceive speech segments and analyze syllables into phonemes. Some studies have shown that being able to discriminate sound parts of words is comparable to or more important than I.Q. scores in first-grade reading success (Robeck and Wilson 1974). It appears, then, that recognizing and knowing the sounds of a language in addition to being able to distinguish them in speech are necessary prerequisites for learning to read.

Although there is disagreement on the importance of auditory-discrimination skills to reading, most educators agree that these skills play some role in the beginning-reading process. A research study (Marzano 1976) has shown that this skill even influences older and more mature readers. In studies that have compared good versus poor readers, the latter group has consistently scored lower on auditory-discrimination tests. Therefore, in order to help prevent poor readers, it seems that developing auditory skills should be part of a preventive therapy program.

One group of children who have been identified repeatedly as poor readers in English-based classrooms and as reading below grade level are children from Spanish-speaking backgrounds. A large portion of their poor reading achievement can be attributed to not having full knowledge of English-language structures. Part of this behavior is reflected in their ability (or inability) to discriminate English sounds that differ from those found in Spanish. Since auditory-discrimination skills seem to affect future reading success, then it has particular significance for Spanish-speaking children. Such children who are learning to read English would appear to be likely candidates for future reading problems due in part to auditory-discrimination confusions. The present study was designed with this thought in mind. It investigated whether teaching Spanish-speaking children to discriminate preselected English sounds would help them to associate those sounds more easily with their corresponding English graphemes.

STATEMENT OF THE PROBLEM

Spanish-speaking children may find it difficult, because of phonological differences between Spanish and English, to discriminate auditorily and to associate with their printed symbols certain English phonemes. Their difficulty in hearing and producing some English sounds may have an adverse effect in learning reading skills such as making sound-letter associations and in reading words with highly similar phonemes.

PURPOSE OF THE STUDY

This study had two purposes. One was to investigate whether or not an ear-training program would help Spanish-speaking children discriminate between pairs of English words which contrasted minimally with sounds identified as difficult for them. The other was to determine whether or not an ear-training program would help Spanish-speaking children more easily make sound-letter associations in a follow-up phonics training program. It was hypothesized that an auditory-discrimination training program would help Spanish-speaking children to better discriminate sounds identified as difficult for them and that it would also improve their ability to learn and use phonics.

HYPOTHESES TESTED

In order to accomplish the purpose of this study, the following null hypotheses were designed:

Hypothesis 1. There will be no significant difference in performance on an auditory-discrimination test between Spanish-speaking children who participate in an ear-training program that teaches sounds identified as difficult for them and Spanish-speaking children who do not receive such training.

Hypothesis 2. There will be no significant difference between Spanish-speaking children who participate in an ear-training program and children who do not receive such training in their ability to discriminate on an auditory-discrimination test the taught pairs of sounds.

Hypothesis 3. There will be no significant difference in the ability to make phoneme-grapheme associations for the sound-letter associations taught between Spanish-speaking children who participate in an auditory-discrimination and a phonics training program and children who receive phonics training only.

Hypothesis 4. There will be no significant difference in the ability to read words containing the sound-letter associations taught between Spanish-speaking children who participate in an auditory-discrimination and a phonics training program and children who receive phonics training only.

Hypothesis 5. Two weeks after a phonics posttest, there will be no significant difference in the ability to retain the taught sound-letter associations between Spanish-speaking children who participate in an auditory-discrimination and a phonics training program and children who receive phonics training only.

DEFINITION OF TERMS

The terms used in the study are operationally defined in the following manner:

- *Auditory discrimination* is the ability to listen to pairs of words presented auditorily and to indicate whether they are identical or different. This ability was measured by performance on an auditory-discrimination test which was administered to the subjects as a pre- and a posttest.

- *Auditory-discrimination training program* is used interchangeably with *ear-training program.* The training program consisted of meeting with experimental subjects four days a week for four weeks. Only oral means were used in teaching subjects to listen to and discriminate between four pairs of consonant sounds. The pairs of sounds taught were the sounds for *ch-sh, b-v, l-ld, s-st.*

- *Phoneme* refers to the smallest unit of sound which, if changed, will change meaning (e.g., *robe-rove*).

- *Spanish-speaking children* in this study refers to children who were able to respond in Spanish to the investigator's satisfaction to all questions of a Spanish-proficiency test.

- *Phonics training program* refers to teaching experimental and control subjects the sound-letter association for the same pairs of sounds as those taught in the ear-training program.

- *Sound-letter association* refers to the ability to discriminate English sounds and associate them with their corresponding letter (grapheme).

STATISTICAL ANALYSIS OF DATA

The auditory-discrimination posttest, the two phonics posttests, and the two phonics-retention tests were analyzed by one-way analysis of covariance with the auditory-discrimination pretest as the covariate. The pretest served as a basic measure of the subjects' initial skills to discriminate sounds. Posttest scores then determined the subjects' improvement due to the training programs. Therefore, one-way analysis of covariance tested the five hypotheses stated previously.

The data for the auditory-discrimination and phonics tests were also analyzed by considering the subjects in groupings other than control and experimental. In one analysis, subjects in English-based and Spanish-based classroom instruction were compared by using two-way analysis of variance. In another, these two groupings were subdivided into bilingual-experimental, bilingual-control, regular-experimental, and regular-control. Their respective means for all the testings were simply compared in terms of gain from pre- to post-test. (No analysis was used to test for significant differences in gain.) The last analysis compared the percentage of correct responses of the total group for items on the auditory-discrimination pre- and post-tests.

PROCEDURES

Eighteen sound pairs were identified as difficult for Spanish-speaking subjects on the basis of a review of the literature and a pilot study. These sound pairs were the foundation for a two-part auditory-discrimination test which was administered to primary-aged, bilingual, Spanish-speaking subjects in a main study. The subjects were then divided into experimental and control groups. Children in the experimental group participated in a four-week ear-training program which taught them to discriminate differences between four of the sound pairs tested. After the training program, control and experimental subjects were given the same auditory-discrimination pretest as a posttest. Two weeks later, all subjects were given a two-part phonics pretest. In order to determine if the ear-training program affected the ability of experimental subjects to associate the sounds taught with their corresponding graphemes, both experimental and control goups participated in a four-week phonics training program. At the end of this training program, all subjects were administered the same two-part phonics pretest as a posttest. Two weeks after the posttests, the subjects were given the same tests as retention tests. The results of the tests were analyzed by one-way analysis of covariance. Since the subjects attended two different schools (one with an English-based regular curriculum and the other with a Spanish-based bilingual curriculum), the data were also analyzed by considering subjects in regular and bilingual classroom groupings.

FINDINGS

The auditory-discrimination posttest was analyzed from three perspectives: total score, sounds taught, and sounds not taught. On all three analyses, the experimental group performed significantly better than the control group (p=.05). These results showed that the ear-training program was effective in helping Spanish-speaking children more easily discriminate English sounds identified as difficult for them. The effectiveness of the four-week training program was apparent, not only for the sounds taught but also for the twenty-four pairs of sounds which were not part of the teaching program. Therefore, helping the experimental subjects to focus on discriminating English sound contrasts that were confusing for them also helped the subjects to listen more closely to word pairs with non-taught contrasting sounds.

The differences in performance of experimental and control subjects on the auditory-discrimination pre- and posttests can be analyzed from several aspects. These include comparing standard deviations, minimum scores, and means. The standard deviation for control subjects on the total pretest score was 3.58, while that of the experimental subjects was 6.42. After the training program, the degree of variability reflected in the standard deviations reversed to 3.95 and 6.06 for experimental and control, respectively. This demonstrated that the children who received ear training became a more homogenous group in their listening skills, while control subjects became more variable. In comparing minimum scores from pre- to posttests, that of the experimental group increased by eleven points on the posttest while that of the control group decreased by one point. In comparing means, the control group had a higher pretest mean (20.50) than experimental subjects (19.28). Posttest results showed that the mean for subjects with ear training increased by nine points (28.42) whereas the mean for those without ear training increased by approximately three points (23.75).

In analyzing the means, standard deviations, and minimum scores for the sounds taught and the sounds not taught, the performances of the two groups on pre- and posttests is similar to that of the total score. In both of these analyses, the standard deviation improved for experimental subjects but worsened for control. The minimum scores for the two analyses improved substantially on the posttest for the experimental group but only slightly or negatively for the control group.

Analysis of the data showed there was no significant difference between groups on either of the two phonics posttests or the retention tests. Therefore, null hypotheses 3, 4, and 5 were retained. These analyses indicate that the auditory-discrimination training program had no effect on the experimental subjects' abilities to learn phonics.

Some evidence is available that suggests experimental subjects were helped in phonics by the auditory-discrimination training program. On the phonics-word pretest, the experimental group had a higher mean than the control group. A t-test analysis of the means showed that the difference between the two approached significance at the .07 level. If the phonics-word pretest had been given at the beginning of the study, it is possible that experimental subjects would have had a lower mean on this test since they had the lower mean on the auditory-discrimination pretest (19.28 versus 20.50 for control). The higher mean of the experimental subjects on the phonics-word pretest could be the result of the ear-training program, particularly because the overall English-speaking skills of experimental subjects were not as strong as those of control subjects. In examining the phonics-word posttest, the means for the two groups increased slightly, with the experimental group maintaining the higher mean (20.42 versus 19.87). It is possible that the auditory-discrimination training program helped experimental subjects score their maximum level on the phonics-word pretest and that this level remained the same on the phonics-word posttest.

CONCLUSIONS

Based on findings of the present study, the following conclusions can be stated:

1. The auditory-discrimination skills of bilingual Spanish-speaking subjects can be improved significantly after a four-week ear-training program.

2. An ear-training program was found to have a transfer effect, as the subjects learned not only to discriminate the sounds taught more readily, but also sounds not taught.

3. Experimental subjects from the bilingual (Spanish-taught) classroom were found to make the most improvement in gain score from auditory-discrimination pre- to posttests over children from the regular classroom. Since bilingual-classroom children were judged to be dominant Spanish speakers, their larger gain scores implied that they have a greater need for ear-training instruction than regular classroom children who speak English and Spanish on a more equal basis.

4. Children who are dominant Spanish speakers were found to be better subjects for studies of learning problems caused

by Spanish-language interference in an English-based curriculum than children who are balanced bilinguals.

5. Subjects from the bilingual classroom were found to have better auditory-discrimination skills because they outperformed (in terms of gain score) regular classroom subjects on the auditory-discrimination posttest. This was perhaps due to the English as a Second Language instruction that bilingual-classroom subjects received on a daily basis.

6. In general, all subjects had phonological problems with English sound discriminations as predicted for Spanish speakers in a contrastive analysis of the two languages.

7. Spanish-speaking children in Kansas had similar difficulties in discriminating certain predicted English sounds as children in Texas, New York City, and New Jersey in studies by Wist (1968), Sardy (1969), and Springer (1975), respectively. In particular, Spanish-speaking children in Kansas found it difficult auditorily to distinguish differences between the sound pair [v] - [b].

8. In general, the ear-training program which consisted of daily instruction for four weeks produced satisfactory results in improving auditory-discrimination skills. This is supported by the significant increase in gain scores by the experimental subjects on the auditory-discrimination test.

9. The higher mean on the phonics-word pretest indicated that improved auditory-discrimination skills of experimental subjects were operational in the subjects' phonic analysis of words. It is felt that the design of the study was such that the effect of the ear-training program on learning phonics was not completely evaluated. Better evidence of the interrelationship between ear training and phonics might have been obtained if the phonics pretest had been given before instead of after the ear-training program.

10. A comparison of subjects in regular classrooms and in bilingual classrooms showed that the means of the two groups differed significantly in four phonics-tests analyses. This suggested that, whenever possible, subjects from only one type of classroom should be used in experimental studies. Subjects who are Spanish dominant will probably show greater improvement on a phonics test since their previous knowledge of English sounds and English sound-letter associations is likely to be less than Spanish-speaking students who speak English more fluently.

Implications

An intensive auditory-discrimination training program emphasizing difficult English sounds should be a part of the regular reading curriculum for Spanish-speaking children in grades K-2 prior to or simultaneous with phonics instruction, in order to help equalize the language skills of these children to those of monolingual English speakers.

A more intensive or longer training program than used in the present study is necessary to develop ear sensitivity to sounds that are particularly difficult for Spanish-speaking children to discriminate. Therefore, teachers should be flexible with regard to time and intensity in implementing an ear-training program. Teachers should not necessarily strive for consistency of time in teaching all sound pairs, as was done in this study.

REFERENCES

Dechant, Emerald V. *Improving the Teaching of Reading*. 2nd ed., pp. 17-204. Englewood Cliffs, N.J.: Prentice-Hall, 1970.

Gibson, E.J., and Levin, H. *The Psychology of Reading*. Pp. 227-63. Cambridge, Mass.: The MIT Press, 1975.

Harris, L.A., and Smith, C.B. *Reading Instruction*. 2nd ed., pp. 28-136. New York: Holt, Rinehart and Winston, 1976.

Marzano, R., et al. "Sound Discrimination and Reading Comprehension in Middle School Students." *Journal of Reading* 20 (1976): 34-36.

Robeck, M.C., and Wilson, J.A. *Psychology of Reading: Foundations of Instruction*. Pp. 201-29. New York: John Wiley and Sons, 1974.

Sardy, Susan J. "Dialect, Auditory Discrimination, and Phonic Skills." Ed.D. dissertation, Yeshiva University, 1969.

Savin, Harris B. "What the Child Knows about Speech When He Starts to Learn to Read." In *Language by Ear and by Eye*, edited by J.F. Kavanagh and I.G. Mattingly, pp. 319-26. Cambridge, Mass.: The MIT Press, 1972.

Shuy, R.W. "Some Language and Cultural Differences in a Theory of Reading." In *Language and Reading*, edited by D.V. Gunderson, pp. 72-87. Washington, D.C.: Center for Applied Linguistics, 1970.

Springer, Judith A. *Auditory Discrimination and Reading Achievement of Puerto Rican Spanish-Speaking First-Grade Children*. Educational Resources Information Center, ERIC ED 109 635, January 1975.

Wist, Ann Hope. "Auditory Discrimination Abilities of Disadvantaged Children in the Primary Grades." Master's thesis, University of Texas at Austin, 1968.

Availability as a Measure of the Oral Spanish Lexicon of the Pre-K and K Chicano Child in Tucson, Arizona

William James Fisher

Semifinalist, Outstanding Dissertations
National Advisory Council on Bilingual Education

Degree conferred August 1977
University of New Mexico
Albuquerque, New Mexico

Dissertation Committee:
Miles Zintz, *Chair*
Dean Brodkey
Rodney W. Young

About the Author

Dr. William James Fisher is currently the principal of Roberts Elementary School in Tucson, Arizona. His professional experience has included teaching at the elementary, junior high, and college levels; teaching English as a Second Language (ESL) to adults; and serving as a consultant to numerous bilingual education programs in Arizona. Dr. Fisher is a member of the National Association for Bilingual Education (NABE) and Teachers of English to Speakers of Other Languages (TESOL). He has served previously as president of the Arizona Bilingual Council (ABC). His membership in the Arizona Association of Mexican-American Educators earned him the "Educator of the Year" award in 1975; and the Arizona Parent Teachers Association presented Dr. Fisher with the "Educator of the Year" award in 1977.

ABSTRACT

The purposes of this study were:

1. To use availability as a method for eliciting Spanish oral speech representative of young Chicano children.

2. To obtain a corpus of content words that reflect the oral Spanish spoken by a selected population of pre-K and K students in bilingual education programs in Tucson, Arizona.

3. To analyze the corpus of lexical items for phonological variant forms as when compared to standard Spanish and local Spanish and to note how the lexical items reflect the children's cultural and socioeconomic background.

The findings of this study were:

1. The use of "availability" as a method for eliciting Spanish oral speech of young Chicano children was found to be feasible. "Availability" is a method for sampling the ready availability of content words in given situational contexts familiar to the children.

2. Content words reflecting the oral Spanish spoken by the pre-K and K students in bilingual education programs in Tucson, Arizona, were obtained. These content or concrete nouns were of sufficient quantity and quality to conclude that the children understood the questions being asked in Spanish. Most of the words that were produced were those that do not have a high frequency on most vocabulary lists.

3. The phonological variant forms used by the children reflected "baby talk," dialectical variations, and other deviations from standard Spanish. The lexical items produced did give an indication of the cultural and socioeconomic background of the Spanish-speaking children in Tucson, Arizona.

STATEMENT OF THE PROBLEM

A serious lack of appropriate bilingual education materials holds back progress in upgrading the Mexican American child's education. Because of the newness of bilingual programs that affect the Spanish-speaking child in the U.S., educators in the Southwest have had to depend on materials created for students outside the United States. Most of the materials in current use in bilingual programs come from Mexico, Puerto Rico, Spain, or South America. These materials were

43

developed for monolingual children from that particular country and reflect linguistic and cultural biases peculiar to that country or locale. Materials specifically designed for the Mexican American or Chicano child in the United States are needed if what the child brings to school is to be reinforced and nurtured. Materials that mirror and value what the child is should have a local flavor—a flavor that is linguistically and culturally relevant to that child. How many times have educators heard and used the statement, "Take the child where he is and build upon that"? If they believe that statement, then they must first find out (1) where the child is, (2) what his culture is, and (3) what his vernacular is.

One common practice in bilingual programs is to take an English vocabulary list and translate it into Spanish. Vocabulary lists have been used by teachers for many years, and they are good tools for the teacher who knows how to use these lists. No literature exists which justifies taking an English vocabulary list, translating it into Spanish, and expecting that the translated version will serve the purpose of the original list.

Vocabulary lists are made for particular languages. They are usually based on frequency and range counts. They are divided so that one can retrieve the first one hundred, two hundred, or any other number of words that one needs or wants. Furthermore, these lists are compiled from many different sources, such as the vocabulary of adults, children, and adolescents; radio announcements; and the written language in newspapers, magazines, novels, and other kinds of books. Examples of these kinds of frequency lists include those of Thorndike and Lorge (1921), Horn (1926), Dolch (1936), Rinsland (1950), and Kučera and Francis (1967). What is obtained in each case is a frequency count that reduces a corpus to a set of frequencies in which there is a relation to the other frequencies. The words at the top of the list occur with high frequency, and the first 250 words may represent as much as 80 percent of a text or speech. This leaves only 20 percent for all the other words. Abstract, grammatical, or general-use words are the most frequently occurring words in English. The grammatical words are frequent because it is impossible to produce a sentence without them. Both grammatical and abstract words have a variety of meanings and many opportunities to occur in any given text (Richards 1970). However, a serious problem remains. "For the language teacher it means that some of the most teachable words—the concrete nouns—may be the least accessible, occurring in the third, fourth, or fifth thousand range rather than within the first few hundred words" (Richards, p. 88). For this reason, this study has focused on concrete nouns in Spanish rather than the most frequent function words.

Tools to assess the oral Spanish language of the Spanish-speaking Mexican American child are lacking. These tools, researched and standardized, can lead to the development of relevant materials for the classroom teacher. Not only can these tools serve assessment purposes, but they also can help the teacher who may not be fluent in the local language to teach a list of common words needed by the children to live in their area or community.

The tool used in this study is called an "availability" measure. It is a method for sampling the ready availability of content words in given situational contexts familiar to the child. It focuses entirely on the world of the child in and out of school and is not dependent on limited in-classroom impressions by the teacher.

PURPOSE OF THE STUDY

The purposes of this study are:
1. To use "availability" as a method for eliciting Spanish oral speech representative of young Chicano children.
2. To obtain a corpus of content words that reflect the oral Spanish spoken by a selected population of the pre-K and K students in bilingual education programs in Tucson, Arizona.
3. To analyze the corpus of lexical items for phonological variant forms when compared to standard Spanish and local Spanish and to note how the lexical items reflect the children's cultural and socioeconomic background.

DEFINITION OF TERMS

The following terms were used throughout this study:
- *Availability:* The notion that a word is available if it is always ready to be used and if it comes to mind immediately and naturally when needed (Michea 1953, p. 340). Mackey called it a measure of the potential of the item in a code (Mackey 1969, p. 203).
- *Centers of interest:* Questions that elicit responses—usually nouns—that are associated in the real world (Michea 1953).
- *Chicano:* Term used to identify members of the Mexican American community in the Southwest. In recent years the term has gained wide acceptance among many persons of Mexican ancestry and reflects a group identity and pride in Mexican American culture and heritage. In this study, *Chicano* and *Mexican American* are used interchangeably.

- *Lexical item:* A word or phrasal response which is taken as one single unit of meaning or response (Dimitrijevic 1969, p. 5).
- *Mexican Americans:* Persons who were born in Mexico and now hold United States citizenship or whose parents or more remote ancestors immigrated to the United States from Mexico. It also refers to persons who trace their lineage to Hispanic or Indo-Hispanic forebears who reside within Spanish or Mexican territory that is now part of the southwestern United States (see *Chicano*).
- *Pretryout:* A preliminary administration of test items to a small sample of students from the population on which the test is to be used. This procedure may be highly informal and may involve only the administration of a mimeographed set of items to between fifty and one hundred students (Thorndike 1971).
- *Single linguistic repertoire:* Theoretical view of treating two languages as part of the same repertoire instead of as two distinct entities (Gumperz 1964, p. 140).
- *Spanish-speaking child:* A child who does one or more of the following: speaks Spanish at home; speaks Spanish to his peers; speaks Spanish to his relatives; speaks Spanish to his friends.
- *Word tokens:* Term used by Mackey (1970); identical to "lexical items" (Dimitrijevic 1969).

THEORETICAL FRAMEWORK

As previously stated, vocabulary lists are usually frequency and range types. In *Twenty-Five Centuries of Language Teaching*, Kelly wrote, "Whereas frequency judges the worth of a linguistic unit according to how often it is used, range refines the measure by showing who uses [the lexical item]" (p. 197). Vocabulary lists are gathered from many sources, such as children, adolescents, and adults; newspapers; magazines; books and novels. Vocabulary lists can reflect written, oral, or both written and oral language. Some can be specific vocabulary investigations for a specific function, such as lists of words "for teaching spelling and reading, basic vocabulary for teaching foreign languages, vocabulary for the blind, etc." (Dimitrijevic 1969, p. 1).

To the notion of frequency and range, a new element, availability, is added. As Kelly pointed out:

Availability is a further refinement detailing in what circumstances speakers use units. This important measure was not fully developed until the twentieth century, appearing in the work of the St-Cloud team who developed "Le Français fondamental." Availability is essentially the resolution of a paradox: a person tends to think of many infrequent terms as frequent because his daily activities keep them before his mind. St-Cloud invented the concept of the center of interest to channel this human peculiarity and to elaborate a meaningful language course (p. 197).

He went on to say:

Availability was a natural consequence of the new cultural orientation of language teaching. One of the less desirable results of early appeals to frequency had been neglect of the cultural dimension of language courses, and this in spite of the cultural preoccupations of the late nineteenth century (p. 200).

Availability is the concept of reaching those words that are not necessarily frequent, but which are there when needed. Michea argued that situations call words to mind according to their degree of availability. He said:

An available word is one which, though not necessarily frequent, is always ready for use, and comes to mind when it is needed. It is a word which, belonging to normal association of ideas, emerges whenever such associations come into play. . . . This is why it is possible to attribute to many concrete nouns a degree of availability within a particular association group, whereas statistics based on the analysis of texts are unable to allot them any stable and well-defined place in the order of frequencies (1964, p. 23).

Mackey has done much work in Canada dealing with French and English bilinguals. His studies, especially those dealing with the notion of availability, are very important to the present research. He wrote:

Availability is a measure of the potential of the items in a code. Whereas frequency of textual occurrence is a suitable measure of language forms which must be used, availability is the appropriate measure for words which may be used (1970, p. 203).

How to get to this storehouse of vocabulary is the next step. Mackey suggested that we have the speakers list items according to "semantic fields." This is also referred to by others as "centers of interest" (Richards 1970; Dimitrijevic 1969; Gougenheim 1956; Michea 1953). Each speaker is asked to supply an inventory of items in each conceptual or semantic field. Examples of this include food, housing, parts of the body, animals, etc., in a prescribed language and within a certain length of time.

At this point, Mackey warned of the possibility of the responses not being in the prescribed language. He said:

> In the case of a bilingual population, if one asks for the vocabulary of one language, one may get certain items which really belong to the vocabulary of the bilingual's other language. This may indicate a number of possibilities. The bilingual may know only the item in his other language, or not know to which language the item belongs. Or he may know both items, but remember one of them more readily than the other (1970, pp. 204-5).

These possibilities are exactly those found by Murphy in his study of the Spanish spoken by New Mexicans in Albuquerque, New Mexico. He went on to explain:

> The speech of each bilingual community is a unique combination of elements from multiple sources and must be viewed in sociological perspective. Two phases of language change must be recognized in the development of the particular linguistic codes of bilingual communities: at the stage of *interference* individual bilinguals confuse their language, using words from one while speaking the other; at the state of *integration*, "errors" previously made by individuals become the norm of the community (1972, n.p.).

Murphy's study is of particular interest in that he not only researches Spanish and English as the two languages in contact, but he also uses the concept of availability to arrive at his vocabulary. He even goes further than Mackey by applying other tests to his findings—translatability and acceptability. Since he is looking for the integrated English word tokens in the speech of his Spanish-speaking informants, his testing is a little more sophisticated than Mackey's. As he stated,

> availability isolated words of interest; translatability honed a sharper edge on them and suggested hypotheses to be tested for acceptability; finally, acceptability tests presented sentences for members of the community to react to (1972, pp. 83-84).

Another study dealing with the notion of availability is the work carried out by Richards in which he compared availability and familiarity. It is his conclusion that

> concrete nouns may have unstable and insignificant ranks in a word frequency list, but significant and stable positions in a familiarity list which indicates the degree to which people expect to hear, see, or use words. . . . In availability testing, domains and centers of interest have to be hypothesized . . . although both word familiarity and word availability appear to measure the cultural significance of nouns, the advantage of word familiarity is that it produces a single index for nouns, rather than a number of independent indices (1970, p. 96).

ANALYSIS OF THE STUDY

This section analyzes some of the findings of the study. Phonological, syntactical, and lexical variations are examined. Some comparisons with other research in the area of Spanish oral-speech production by young Mexican American children are discussed. Inferential conclusions regarding socioeconomic status and culture are also included.

Phonological Changes in Children's Speech

One of the common phenomena in the speech patterns of the Spanish-speaking children in Tucson, Arizona, is a form of phonological variation, such as vowel changes, consonant changes, and the elimination of certain sound clusters. The reasons for this phenomenon are difficult to pinpoint. Perhaps in the child's evolving language, these changes or "baby talk" play an important role in the child's transition into adult language. This hypothesis supports those who advocate an earlier entry into a formalized educational setting (preschool programs) for those children who come to school speaking a language other than English.

The present analysis is similar to that of Cornejo (1969) and Stewart (1973). Stewart's findings support those of Cornejo's in that they found patterns of baby talk and numerous examples of significant interference between English and Spanish. Both Stewart and Cornejo found a high frequency of phonological deficiencies in the performance of the Spanish language. They also found that the majority of the children expressed themselves better in English than in Spanish, although a wide range of relative oral Spanish proficiency was demonstrated.

This study supports Stewart's and Cornejo's findings related to the serious deficiencies found in the articulation of common Spanish words. Where this study deviated from theirs was in the lack of evidence for interferences between English and Spanish and ample evidence for adequate Spanish labels, indicating a strong possibility of Spanish-language dominance.

Another basic difference between this study and those mentioned above was the use of the Spanish language. Cornejo and Stewart did a comparison of production in English/Spanish, while in the present study, an analysis of the Spanish language was the only consideration.

The methodology also differed. Where Cornejo and Stewart used visual cues to elicit speech, this study used only verbal stimuli to elicit language. It was the belief of this researcher that verbal, open-ended stimuli would elicit more responses in the dominant language in a freer, nonrestrictive situation, without the possibility of right-wrong responses and nonfamiliar cues used as stimuli.

Baby Talk. Mention was made concerning baby talk and how Cornejo and Stewart found many instances of this phenomenon in their studies of young children. They drew on many of the characteristics enumerated in Ferguson's study (1964).

While it can be expected that four- and five-year-olds will use baby talk in many instances, it is difficult to place words in this category with any degree of certainty. There are other things to consider. Are the children modeling adult speech? Are they repeating what siblings speak? Could they be hearing the speech of uneducated Spanish speakers?

Before we classify a word as being an example of baby talk, more research is needed. We must know what to expect as baby talk when we have two languages in contact, in this case English and Spanish. The best way would be to test children in northern Mexico to find out what their baby talk is and compare this with the findings in Tucson.

If one is comparing lists of words labelled baby talk and dialect, a point to remember is that baby talk is a maturation process and should disappear as the child becomes older. If one is talking about dialect, chances are great that this variation will not be lost due to age but will continue into adulthood.

The following are some category responses of baby talk given by the students in this study. These characteristics are from a study by Ferguson (1964).

1. Use of the diminutive
2. Reduction of phonemes
3. Addition of phonemes

4. Vowel simplification and elimination of diphthong
5. Elimination of final phoneme
6. Reduction of initial syllable
7. Phonemic reduction within a word
8. Phonemic changes

Dialectal variations. Some children's responses reflected common dialectal variations. They produced pronunciation differences which are characteristic of northern Sonora and southern Arizona adult Spanish speech.

Loan blends. Loan blend is a new idiom which develops in a language as a result of borrowing—one element is borrowed, the other is native but is adapted to the loan original (Cornejo 1969). Cornejo finds this phenomenon in Texas, sometimes referred to as *pochismos* (Barker 1972). Reference is also made to the study by Teschner (1972) dealing with Chicago Mexican Spanish.

Analogy. Some new forms based on linguistic correspondence were noted (Cornejo 1969). The children have adopted the frequently occurring English plural *-es*. The children gave the standard Spanish and variant forms.

Alien words. Alien words are borrowed words that still retain part of the phonemic pattern, stress, written form, etc., of the language of origin (Cornejo 1969).

Metathesis. A change of the order of elements occurred within the words (Cornejo 1969). The young informants gave both standard Spanish and variant forms.

Pure loan words. These words are used by many children and adults in everyday conversations. Because some words may not have a Spanish equivalent, the Spanish speaker easily borrows these words from English speakers. These are usually referred to as Anglicisms. Haugen (1953) described these as "pure loan words," i.e., borrowings which consist of free or bound morphemes imported directly from the "lending" into the "borrowing" language.

Spanish-English mix. While the samples of Spanish-English mix are not numerous, there is an indication that some informants are using Spanish syntax when giving responses whereas others give expressions in which English syntax prevails. Clearly the children mix the two languages. This study does not address itself to the question of language dominance, since the children were asked to respond in Spanish and not in the two languages.

Cultural Implications

The language of the home was clearly indicated in the words the children volunteered. Games that children play give some indication of their cultural background. Games like *Rueda de San Miguel, A la víbora, Matarile, Naranja dulce, Huevo perdido,* and *El diablo y la monja* are typical of the types of games that children from a Mexican background play. Others are universal games that most children play, except that these use Spanish words. Some examples of these are *colegio, coludos, chota, casa, mama,* and *comadres.*

The children gave many family-member names in the study. The concept of the extended family seems to be very much alive in the homes of the children that were interviewed. *Abuelo, abuela, nanas, tatas,* and *abuelitas* are names for grandparents and are mentioned forty-two times. Seventy *father* and eighty-three *mother* responses indicate a fairly stable family unit. Forty-six informants name brothers or sisters as persons who live in a family. This small response is attributed to many of the children being offspring of young mothers with only one child or being the first child.

Foods originating in Mexico are a common fare in Tucson. *Salsa de chile* and *pico* are commonly eaten by Mexican families. Preference for *caldo, cazuela, menudo, sopa, cocido,* and *pozole* usually indicate from what region of Mexico a family came. They are souplike dishes with distinct flavors. *Burros* are not animals, but the original Mexican sandwich, made by wrapping almost anything with a flour tortilla. *Nopales* are made from the young new leaves of the *nopal* plant, a variety of desert cactus. Prepared and cooked, they taste much like string beans. *Nopales* can be mixed with many things, especially eggs and chile. *Chorizo* and *chorizo con papas* are very common choices for a hearty breakfast. *Chorizo* is a highly seasoned mixture of meat and red chile. It may be bought in sausage form or as ground sausage meat. *Tortillas* are made from *maíz* or flour. Flour *tortillas* are more common in the area of the study. *Sandwich* and *torta* are used by some children to mean the same thing—two pieces of bread with something in between.

Although it was not the intent of this study to compare this list of words with any other study, it is interesting to note that all the words that are starred (*) in Table 2 are found in Cornejo's study. A comparison between lists cannot be made because Cornejo's list uses a frequency of *one* or more while this study uses a frequency of *twenty* or more. To do a comparison, all the words would have to be compared with those in Cornejo's study.

Table 1
Vocabulary Frequency of Response

#1	manos	76	#7	frijoles	43	#17	carrito	44
	cabeza	53		carne	41		muñeca	28
	pies	47		sopa	36			
	ojos	26		huevo	33	#18	dulces	43
	boca	22		papas	21		comida	33
	dedos	22						
	brazos	21	#8	leche	101	#19	azul	68
	patas	20		agua	93		rojo	49
	piernas	20		juice	21		amarillo	47
							verde	47
#2	ojos	94	#9	platos	70		anaranjado	33
	boca	90		comida	60		café	32
	nariz	89		cuchara	48		morado	25
	dientes	30		tenedor	37		colorado	24
	oído	25		cuchillo	27		negro	23
	orejas	22						
			#10	sillas	41	#20	uno	89
#3	pantalón	89		mesas	34		dos	87
	zapatos	73		juguetes	31		cinco	83
	vestido	71		libros	28		cuatro	82
	blusa	30					tres	78
	camisa	29	#11	carro	88			
	calcetines	27		bus	38	#21	carro	78
	shorts	22		troque	37		bicicletas	40
				avión	24			
#4	estufa	45		caballo	22	#22	perfume	42
	comida	44					flores	41
	mesa	38	#12	perro	46			
	platos	34		gatos	36	#23	silla	96
	silla	29		caballo	31		sofá	30
	trastes	28		elefante	28		sillón	28
	vasos	22		león	20		cama	26
#5	excusado	61	#13	carros	29	#24	lavar	62
	jabón	57		muñecas	26		limpiar	62
	agua	42		pelota	25		barrer	36
	baño	31		bicicletas	24		mapear	26
	toallas	31						
			#14	tienda	22	#25	mamá	81
#6	sillón	43					papá	70
	mesa	39	#15	trabajar	25		nana	23
	sofá	39					hermana	22
	televisión	35	#16	vasos	105			
	sillas	32		boca	44			
				tazas	34			
				copas	25			

N = 100

Table 2
List of Words Having a Frequency of 20 or More—Alphabetized

agua*	elefante	pantalón*
amarillo*	estufa*	papa
anaranjado	excusado*	papá*
avión		pata
azul*	flor*	pelota*
	frijol*	perfume
baño		perro*
barrer	gato*	pie*
bicicleta*		pierna*
blusa	hermana*	plato*
boca*	huevo	
brazo		rojo
bus*	jabón*	
	juguete*	shorts
caballo*	juice	silla*
cabeza		sillón*
café*	lavar*	sofá*
calcetín*	leche*	sopa
cama	león	
camisa	libro	taza*
carne*	limpiar*	televisión
carrito*		tenedor
carro*	mamá*	tienda*
cinco	mano*	toalla
colorado*	mapear	trabajar*
comida*	mesa*	traste*
copa	morado	tres*
cuatro*	muñeca*	troque*
cuchara*		
cuchillo*	nana	uno*
	nariz	
dedo*	negro	vaso*
diente*		verde*
dos*	oído	vestido*
dulce*	ojo*	
	oreja	zapato*

N = 100

*Indicates words appearing in Ricardo Cornejo's study "Bilingualism: Study of the Lexicon of the Five-Year-Old Spanish Speaking Children of Texas."

Socioeconomics

The extended family concept, attributable in part to cultural patterns of the Mexican American, can also be attributed to socioeconomic level. Tucson is a crossroads in the stream of migrant people from Mexico, be they legal or illegal immigrants. Their first stop in the United States may be to see a relative or friend. Many families who choose to come to the United States may live with other adults until they can find a permanent job or more suitable quarters. It is not uncommon to find a home which consists of grandfather, grandmother, mother, father, an aunt or uncle, and four or five children, often sharing a one- or two-bedroom house.

Some of the responses given by the children in the study presented a dichotomy; they gave responses such as *hoyo donde hacen caca, tina, pompa*, and *hielero*, which indicate a low socioeconomic level, and also responses such as *máquina de lavar, lavatrastes, piano, consola*, and *teléfono*, which indicate a higher socioeconomic level.

The areas in which the two schools are located are considered low socioeconomic areas, but there are many homes that are considered low middle class. Some homes, though old, are nonetheless well maintained.

There are still some homes that have outside plumbing and dirt floors. Some of the families do not own their homes and must pay rent. This accounts for answers to some of the questions that give the impression of a one- or two-room home.

Explanation of Tables

Table 1 presents the vocabulary reponses having a frequency of 20 or more. Table 2 is an alphabetized list. Duplicated words are omitted, and words are presented in the singular form, decreasing the word list from 110 to 90.

MAIN FINDINGS

In general, much has been written about the need for better instruments to assess the bilingual child. By using instruments designed as this one was, more information about the oral language of Spanish speaking children in the Southwest can be obtained.

Vocabulary lists based on oral production appear to be a practical method of obtaining word lists. Most of the other word lists used by teachers are derived by compiling words used in written communications. There have been some attempts in the past to produce vocabulary lists that reflect the oral speech of Spanish-speaking students in the United States.

The corpus of lexical items obtained by the instrument is certainly extensive, indicating that the subjects examined had a wide range of command of the Spanish language. However, whether they are English or Spanish dominant was not the purpose of this study; this study sought only to compile a list of concrete nouns in Spanish.

The present research was an attempt to arrive at those words which appear very low on most word lists. The reason for this is that the most frequently used words are those with an abstract, grammatical, or general use. These may represent 80 percent of a text or speech. The concepts of availability and centers of interest do produce noun responses. This corroborates the research of Dimitrijevic (1969).

CONCLUSIONS

Oral speech can be obtained using the concepts of availability and centers of interest, as was done in this study.

Baby talk is common among the subjects interviewed. More research is needed to be able to ascertain the reasons for this phenomenon.

Other phonological variants are also common, but archaisms are not. Metathesis, analogies, loan words, and dialect responses were noted in this study. What were not found were responses that could be classified as archaisms. In Cornejo's study with children from Texas, this type of response was noted. Studies done in New Mexico usually elaborate about archaisms, which are very common in the speech of the native speakers of Spanish (Kercheville 1934; Tireman 1948). The lack of archaic forms in the Spanish spoken by Tucsonans was also noted by Barker (1972). He further characterized the local Spanish as similar to that of northern Sonora, Mexico.

The children of the two bilingual schools in Tucson, Arizona, seem to have a good command of the Spanish language. Since the children in the study were able to understand the questions and to give appropriate concrete-noun responses, this would certainly be an indication of their command of the language. When discrepancies from standard Spanish were found, they were at the phonological level.

There appears to be some interference between English and Spanish, although the samples elicited were not of sufficient quantity to be conclusive.

The young Spanish-speaking Chicano child responds in both English and Spanish when asked questions in Spanish. The reason for this is not clear. It may be that at four to six years of age, communication skills are such that the child only knows how to communicate and may not be fully aware that he/she has two language systems.

RECOMMENDATIONS

The instrument developed to elicit Spanish oral speech that is representative of young Chicano children does accomplish its task, but certain modifications are recommended. These recommendations were made by those who helped administer the instrument.

1. Reduce the number of questions to fifteen. Twenty-five questions are too many to administer to small children at one session.
2. Eliminate question number 15. This question confused the young children. It also necessitates dividing the lexical items into *ser* and *hacer*. The purpose of the study was to elicit noun responses and not verb responses.
3. The sessions with the children should be tape-recorded. Although Spanish has a high correlation between phoneme and grapheme, and examiners are able to record the children's sound patterns, a recording would allow for checking when there is a question involving certain pronunciations.
4. Those questions that deal mostly with the home environment should be asked in the child's home. Those questions having to do with the school setting, are best asked in the school. It might be possible to devise separate questionnaires to be given at home and at school.

Implications

The instrument developed in this study, and other single-purpose instruments, if administered to all children that come to our schools speaking Spanish as a first language, could serve to obtain a continually growing and changing list of lexical items. Such a list would serve various purposes. For example, it would be useful as—

1. a compilation of a common Spanish lexicon typical of young children;
2. an instrument by which teachers could become familiar with the Spanish vernacular of their Chicano students;
3. a guide in preparing Spanish written materials to be used in the classroom;

4. a checklist of errors in pronunciation common to young Chicano students;
5. a diagnostic classroom tool when working with children who speak Spanish;
6. a teaching tool for those who are preparing teachers to work with Chicano students.

Further studies in the usefulness of function words is recommended. Data could be gathered, in part, by using the present instrument. Then some notion of overall competence in Spanish might be attempted.

Since children model adult speech patterns, future research should address itself to the relationship between dialect and baby talk. In the present study, it was difficult to distinguish between those two types of responses.

On a national level, bilingual educators urgently need adequate materials reflecting the language and culture of the Spanish-speaking populations, be they Chicano, Cubano, Puerto Riqueño, etc.

It is hoped that by using instruments that measure the oral ability of young Spanish-speaking students, adequate teaching materials, written in the language they hear and speak, will go far in making the educational process truly responsive to the needs of a long-neglected segment of the school population—the Spanish-speaking child.

APPENDIX

Questions Involving the Centers of Interest
for Pre-K and K Children

1. ¿Cuáles son las partes del cuerpo?
2. ¿Cuáles son las partes de la cara que sabes?
3. ¿Qué ropa se ponen las niñas? ¿Qué ropa se ponen los niños?
4. ¿Cuáles son las cosas que hay en una cocina?
5. ¿Cuáles son las cosas que hay en el baño?
6. ¿Cuáles son las cosas que se ven en la sala de una casa?
7. ¿Qué cosas te gusta comer?
8. ¿Qué cosas te gusta tomar cuando tienes sed?
9. ¿Qué cosas se ponen en la mesa cuando vamos a comer?
10. ¿Qué cosas hay en la escuela?
11. ¿En qué cosas puedes viajar o montar para ir de un lugar a otro?
12. ¿Cuáles son los animales que más te gustan?
13. ¿Cuáles son los juegos que más te gusta jugar?
14. ¿Cuáles son los lugares que más te gustaría ir a ver en el pueblo?
15. Cuando seas grande ¿qué te gustaria ser?
16. ¿Qué cosas puedes usar para tomar agua?
17. ¿Qué juguetes te gustaría que te compraran?
18. ¿Qué cosas te gusta comprar en la tienda?
19. ¿Cuáles son los colores que más te gustan?
20. ¿Cuáles son los números que sabes?
21. ¿Qué cosas tienen rueditas?
22. ¿Qué cosas tienen olor?
23. ¿En qué cosas te puedes sentar?
24. ¿Cómo le ayudas a tu mamá en la casa?
25. ¿Cuáles son las personas que viven en una familia?

REFERENCES

Barker, George C. *Pachuco: An American-Spanish Argot and Its Social Functions in Tucson, Arizona.* Tucson: University of Arizona Press, 1970.

———. *Social Functions of Language in a Mexican-American Community.* Anthropological Papers of the University of Arizona, no. 22. Tucson: University Press, 1972.

Cornejo, Ricardo J. "Bilingualism: Study of the Lexicon of the Five-Year-Old Spanish Speaking Children of Texas." Ph. D. dissertation, University of Texas at Austin, 1969.

Dimitrijevic, Naum R. *Lexical Availability.* Heidelberg, Germany: Julius Groos Verlag, 1969.

Dolch, E.W., and Buckingham, B.R. *A Combined Word List.* Boston: Ginn and Company, 1936.

Ferguson, Charles A. "Baby Talk in Six Languages." In *The Ethnography of Communication,* edited by John J. Gumperz and Dell Hymes. *American Anthropologist* 66, no. 6 (1964), pt. II, pp. 103-14.

Gougenheim, G., et al. *L'elaboration du Français Fondamental.* Paris: Dider, 1956.

Gumperz, John J. "Linguistic and Social Interaction in Two Communities." *American Anthropologist* 66, no. 2 (1964), pp. 137-53.

Haugen, Einar. *The Norwegian Language in America.* 2 vols. Philadelphia: University of Pennsylvania Press, 1953.

Horn, Ernest. *A Basic Writing Vocabulary.* Iowa City: State University of Iowa, 1926.

Kelly, Louis G. *Twenty-Five Centuries of Language Teaching.* Rowley, Mass.: Newbury House Publishers, 1969.

Kercheville, F.M. *A Preliminary Glossary of New Mexican Spanish.* University of New Mexico Bulletin, Language Series, vol. 5, no. 3, whole no. 247. Albuquerque: University of New Mexico, 15 July 1934.

Kučera, H., and Francis, W. *Computational Analysis of Present-Day American English.* Providence: Brown University Press, 1967.

Mackey, William F. "Interference, Integration, and the Synchronic Fallacy." In Monograph Series on Languages and Linguistics, no. 23, edited by James Alatis, pp. 195-223. Washington, D.C.: Georgetown University Press, 1970.

———. "Optimalization of the Population-Response Ratio in Lexicometric Sampling." In *Review for Applied Linguistics* 7, pp. 3-47. Louvain, Belgium: 1970.

Michea, M.R. "Basic Vocabulary." *New Research and Techniques for the Benefit of Modern Language Teaching.* Pp. 19-33. Strasbourg: Council for Cultural Cooperation, 1964.

_____. "Mots Frequents et Mots Disponsible." *Les Langues Modernes*, no. 4 (1953), pp. 338-44.

Murphy, Raymond Paul. "Integration of English Lexicon in Albuquerque Spanish." Ph.D. dissertation, University of New Mexico, 1972.

Richards, Jack C. "A Psycholinguistic Measure of Vocabulary Selection." *IRAL* 8, no. 2 (May 1970).

Rinsland, Henry. *A Basic Vocabulary of Elementary School Children.* New York: Macmillan Company, 1950.

Stewart, Adela A. "The Relative Oral Spanish Proficiency (Lexical) of Second Generation Mexican-American Kindergarten Children in Tucson, Arizona." Ph.D. dissertation, University of Arizona, 1974.

Teschner, Richard V. "Anglicisms in Spanish. A Cross-Referenced Guide to Previous Findings, Together with English Lexical Influence on Chicago Mexican Spanish." Ph.D. dissertation, University of Wisconsin, 1972.

Thorndike, E.L., and Lorge, I. *The Teacher's Word Book of 30,000 Words.* New York: Teachers College, Columbia University, 1944.

Thorndike, Robert L. *Educational Measurement.* Washington, D.C.: American Council on Education, 1971.

Tireman, L.S. "Spanish Vocabulary of Four Native Spanish-Speaking Pre-1 Grade Children." University of New Mexico Publications in Education, no. 2 (1948).

Bilingual-Bicultural Instructional Aide Roles as Perceived by Teachers, Administrators, and Instructional Aides

María N. Ortiz

Semifinalist, Outstanding Dissertations
National Advisory Council on Bilingual Education

Degree conferred August 1978
University of the Pacific
Stockton, California

Dissertation Committee:
Augustine García, *Chair*
Armand Maffia
Fe Hufana
Graciela Urteaga
Randall Rockey

About the Author

Dr. María N. Ortiz is a staff member of the California State Department of Education, Office of Bilingual Education. She serves as a consultant whose primary responsibility is in the area of bilingual staff development. Dr. Ortiz has had a variety of professional experiences, which include conducting training sessions on diagnosing reading problems unique to minority children at the elementary level, designing modules for teacher-trainees, and training instructors of high school equivalency math. Her expertise and interest lie in training bilingual teachers and teacher aides.

ABSTRACT

The purpose of the study was to investigate the role of the bilingual-bicultural instructional aide. Variables were studied which are integral to the effectiveness of the bilingual paraprofessional and which reflect the perceptions of teachers, bilingual aides, and administrators currently working in bilingual classroom settings. From the results of the investigation, the role and effectiveness of the bilingual aides could be studied in order to determine meaningful bases for recruitment, hiring, placement, and relevant training.

The major findings and conclusions of the study showed that there were significant differences among the three referent groups in what they perceived to be the ideal and the actual role performance and competence of bilingual-bicultural instructional aides in bilingual classrooms. Specific findings were the following:

1. The role functions of the bilingual aides were perceived differently by each group. The administrators seemed to show more consensus regarding what the ideal functions of the aides should be.
2. Lack of consensus regarding the actual role performance of these bilingual aides was apparently due to many factors. One major factor was probably the lack of communication among those directly involved with the interviewing, hiring, training, and placing of the aides.
3. While the administrators seemed to agree on the relationship between what the aides were doing in the classroom and how competent they were in performing their functions, this was not true for the teachers or the aides. The aides agreed least about their role and seemed to show the least confidence in their abilities to perform their functions.
4. The bilingual-bicultural instructional aides were not performing the specific functions for which they were hired (translating, teaching methodology, and language instruction) because apparently they were not competent. However, only the aides seemed to feel that they were not receiving appropriate training. Both teachers and administrators felt that the aides were adequately trained or being trained.

THE PROBLEM

In response to the problem of limited numbers of credentialed bilingual personnel, many school districts have applied for funds to hire and train bilingual-bicultural teacher aides. The hiring and training of bilingual paraprofessionals, however, has not been simple. Those involved with these tasks have realized that bilingual paraprofessionals generally lack proper training in all areas of teaching methodology, language instruction, and in their own cultural and historical backgrounds (Seymann 1976, p. 6).

Background to the Problem

The problem of lack of trained bilingual paraprofessionals has been complicated by the demanding roles of these paraprofessionals. In most cases, the aides are asked to assume instructional duties before they are given proper training. This is partially due to the immediate need of utilizing their bilingual skills in bilingual situations with monolingual teachers. Godwin (1977, p. 265) states, "The involvement of bilingual paraprofessionals in such a setting is more than a question of titles and duties. Special roles seem to emerge." The bilingual-bicultural aide is asked to play the role of teacher, tutor, playground supervisor, and community liaison because of special bilingual-bicultural skills. But, in most cases, this paraprofessional is not legally responsible to carry out these duties nor adequately trained to perform them effectively (Seymann, pp. 6-8).

Local variations in selection, training, placement, and assessment practices of instructional aides have created variations as to the "proper and legal" role of the bilingual-bicultural paraprofessional in bilingual classrooms. According to a study done in 1973, "legal and pragmatic views show divergence as to what constitutes appropriate functions for aides. The law tends to restrict the aides' functions in the direction of comparatively little contact with students. Practitioners tend to prescribe quasi-instructional roles for the aides" (Barba, p. 5). A study conducted in 1974 revealed that only twenty-three states had laws or state board of education policies defining the legal status of teacher aides (Tollett and Tollett 1974, p. 30).

Studies have found specific problems of overutilization and underutilization of bilingual-bicultural instructional aides due to lack of uniform role definition of functions. Both Barba (p. 7) and Seymann (p. 23) found that bilingual paraprofessionals were given teaching responsibilities for which they were unprepared or ill-trained to perform. The lack of bilingual teachers demanded that bilingual paraprofessionals be put into situations where they assumed teaching duties immediately. Morales (1976) recently found the other extreme to be true. His study revealed that the most frequently performed duties of bilingual aides were clerical duties of duplicating instructional materials and other noninstructional activities. All three authors recommended further studies in order to help delineate the role functions of the bilingual-bicultural paraprofessionals, which could prevent further misuse of their skills.

Differences in perceptions held among teachers, administrators, and instructional aides of the aide's functions in the bilingual classroom also complicate the role of the paraprofessional. There seems to be a lack of agreement among these referent groups in regard to the types of functions and in regard to the frequency with which these functions should occur. Ollio (1971, p. 121) and Zalk et al. (1975) found this to be true in their research. In their studies on teacher aides, they similarly concluded that:

> ...principals, teachers, and teacher aides taken in groups do exhibit a significant level of incongruence to the degree that some specificity needs to be related to the role of the teacher aide . . . a greater degree of compatibility would result if school districts would construct programs involving principals, teachers, and teacher aides. The major thrust of these programs would be to identify the job functions of the teacher aide (Ollio).

> The role of the instructional aide needs to be specified to create the most effective disposition of his/her skills in the classroom. . . . The role of the instructional aide is not well-defined. Training on the role of the instructional aide in the teaching-learning team should be given, as well as lectures on the expectations and limitations of instructional aides. The trainees should be given sufficient orientation to enable them to perform effectively in the classroom (Zalk et al.).

Lack of consensus among those working directly with bilingual aides as to the role and effectiveness of teacher aides is a very serious problem. Lack of research in this area has contributed to the problem, since it is needed to help educators focus on training needs, role assignments, and evaluations of role performance. There is, therefore, a need to conduct studies which specifically deal with the role and effectiveness of these paraprofessionals, at least at the local levels, in order to determine meaningful bases for recruitment, hiring, placement, and relevant training.

Statement of the Problem

The purpose of this study was to investigate the relationship among variables which are integral to the role of the bilingual-bicultural instructional aide, and reflect the perceptions of teachers, teacher aides, and administrators. The study concerned itself with: (1) the role functions of the teacher aide; (2) the frequency with which these functions occur; and (3) the effectiveness of the teacher aide in performing these functions.

In order to accomplish its purpose, the study investigated these areas based on the perceptions of three referent groups: teachers, administrators, and bilingual-bicultural instructional aides working in bilingual-bicultural settings. The study also investigated two significant relationships: (1) assumed role functions and frequency of occurrence of these; and (2) assumed role functions and effectiveness of role performance. From the results of the investigation, the following objectives were to be accomplished:

1. A consensus role definition for the bilingual-bicultural instructional aide would be developed.
2. The discrepancies between the ideal and the actual functions of these paraprofessionals could be reduced.
3. Weak areas of job performance of the bilingual-bicultural instructional aide would be evaluated in order to recommend specific training.

HYPOTHESES

It has been stated that the purpose of this study was to determine the relationship among variables that are integral to the role of the bilingual-bicultural instructional aide. Hypotheses 1, 2, and 3 focused upon intergroup consensus regarding each of these variables.

Hypotheses 4 through 9 were designed to investigate two significant relationships: (1) assumed role functions and frequency of occurrence of these; and (2) assumed role functions and effectiveness of role performance. From these, the discrepancies between the ideal and actual role performance of the aides as perceived within each group could be identified. Hypothesis 10 was included in order to determine any significant influences of biographical variables on the hypotheses.

Hypothesis 1. No significant differences exist among teacher, administrator, and instructional-aide groups in their perceptions of the desirable instructional aide *functions* that should be performed in the bilingual-bicultural classroom.

Hypothesis 2. No significant differences exist among teacher, administrator, and instructional-aide groups in their perceptions regarding the *frequency* of desirable intructional-aide functions.

Hypothesis 3. No significant differences exist among teacher, administrator, and instructional-aide groups in their perceptions of instructional-aide *competence* in performing these functions.

Hypothesis 4. No significant differences exist between teachers' perceptions of desirable instructional-aide functions and teachers' perceptions regarding frequency of desirable instructional-aide functions.

Hypothesis 5. No significant differences exist between administrators' perceptions of desirable instructional-aide functions and administrators' perceptions regarding frequency of desirable instructional-aide functions.

Hypothesis 6. No significant differences exist between instructional aides' perceptions of desirable instructional-aide functions and instructional aides' perceptions regarding frequency of desirable instructional-aide functions.

Hypothesis 7. No significant differences exist between teachers' perceptions of desirable instructional-aide functions and teachers' perceptions regarding the competence of the instructional aide in performing these functions.

Hypothesis 8. No significant differences exist between administrators' perceptions of desirable instructional-aide functions and administrators' perceptions regarding the competence of the instructional aide in performing these functions.

Hypothesis 9. No significant differences exist between instructional aides' perceptions of desirable instructional-aide functions and instructional aides' perceptions regarding the competence of the instructional aide in performing these functions.

Hypothesis 10. No significant relationships exist between the perceptions of desirable instructional-aide functions and the following variables: age, sex, education and/or training, language component, and instructional grade level.

SIGNIFICANCE OF THE STUDY

A review of the literature indicated the need to determine some consensus of role definition for bilingual-bicultural instructional aides in order to improve their effectiveness. This need was evident from the review of the literature, which pointed out diversities in the legal status of aides, inconsistencies about their role functions, and a scarcity of research that has dealt with their perceived role functions and effectiveness of role performance.

The importance of role consensus and role effectiveness is evident in the theories of several researchers.

1. Getzels (1964) found that effective functioning of role behavior of position holders is not likely to occur where role incumbents find themselves exposed to conflicting expectations held by their superiors. He states that effectiveness of role behavior in a social system such as a school depends on the degree of congruence between the perceptions and expectations of the complementary role incumbents.

2. Sarbin (1954, p. 229) contends that individuals appraise the position of others in order to perceive their own status more clearly. They then respond to situations in a manner which they perceive as being appropriate to their jobs among such positions.

3. Barnard's (1966, pp. 44 and 92) theory states that the effectiveness of an organization is related to the degree of congruence between the actual behavior of the employees and the role expectations that their superiors hold for them.

Authorities in the field of bilingual-bicultural instructional-aide training have commented that, when the paraprofessionals in bilingual education are used effectively, individual needs and individual differences of the students are ordinarily met. However, they agree, this cannot be done without relevant training which directs itself to the specific role functions of the instructional aides and to their effectiveness of job performance (Leighton 1969). The results of this study can be used to clearly specify the role functions of bilingual paraprofessionals so that they may perform more effectively. The discrepancies between the ideal and the actual functions of these aides can be reduced. Weak areas in the aides' job performance can be identified in order to recommend specific training. Statistical methods for future evaluations of the aides' performance can be discussed and implemented. The overall findings of this study can be used by the local school districts as a base for preliminary needs assessments from which to plan in-service and preservice training for bilingual-bicultural instructional aides.

DEFINITION OF TERMS

The objectives and procedures of this study required the use of certain technical terms. The following operational definitions are provided to facilitate the usage of these terms in the study:

- *Perceptions:* Bowman and Klopf (1968, p. 5) defined this concept as the awareness and judgments resulting from having observed certain actions.
- *Bilingual-bicultural instructional aide:* The 1976 Bilingual-Bicultural Education Act of California defines this term as "an aide fluent in both English and the primary language of the limited-English-speaking pupil or pupils in a bilingual-bicultural program . . . who is familiar with the cultural heritage of the limited-English-speaking pupils in the bilingual classes to which he or she is assigned (Assembly Bill No. 1329, Chapter 5.76, Bilingual-Bicultural Education Act of 1976, pp. 4-5). In the bilingual classes where this study was conducted, other terms were used for the same role. Those to be used in this study are: bilingual aide, bilingual/cross-cultural teacher aide, bilingual paraprofessional, and bicultural instructional aide. *Bilingual-bicultural instructional aide* will be the main term.
- *Likert-type rating scale:* This scale contains a set of items, all of which are considered approximately equal in attitude or value loading. The subject responds with varying "degrees of intensity" on a scale ranging between extremes such as agree-disagree, always-never, etc. The scores of the responses for each of the separate scales are summed, or summed and averaged, to yield an individual's attitude score (Isaac and Michael 1974, p. 100).
- *Self-report questionnaire:* This is a type of instrument designed to be self-administered by the participants. It is often used in educational research for descriptive studies and in the measurement of attitude and opinion. The questionnaire used in this study was composed of fixed-alternative (closed) items. This was done in order to get uniformity and reliability of responses (ibid., pp. 98-99).
- *Language minority:* This term is used in this study to refer to persons in the United States who speak a non-English native language and who belong to an identifiable minority group. For the purpose of this study, the language-minority groups included were: Mexican Americans, Asian Americans, and Filipino Americans (U.S. Commission on Civil Rights, *A Better Chance to Learn: Bilingual Education*, p. 1).
- *Teacher* and *specialist:* The term *teacher* is used to refer to the professional credentialed person in the classroom. *Specialist* refers to experienced teachers who have specific responsibilities for developing bilingual-bicultural curricula in specific

content areas such as language, ESL, math, etc. In this study, the responses of the teachers and specialists were placed under one category—*teacher* (Assembly Bill No. 1329, p. 4).

- *Bilingual-bicultural classrooms:* These are classrooms in which English and another language are used as instructional media in the educational program. The student's native language and the cultural factors of that language are used as media of instruction, while all necessary skills are introduced, maintained, and developed in the second language and culture.
- *Roles and functions:* "All societies are organized around positions (statuses), and the persons who occupy these positions perform specialized functions or roles. . . . Roles and functions are conjoined. Roles are defined in terms of the functions performed by the person to validate his occupancy of the position" (Sarbin 1954, p. 224). Other terms such as *duties, responsibilities,* and *assignments* are used interchangeably with *functions* and *roles.* In this study, the term *role* is used to refer to the overall concept of specified behaviors, while *functions* is used to refer to those specified behaviors that make up the role.
- *Administrator:* In this study, the term refers to those people who are either building principals or program directors.

SUBJECTS

In order to fulfill the purpose of this study, 150 questionnaires were distributed to the following three referent groups identified for this study: 80 bilingual-bicultural instructional aides, 50 teachers, and 20 administrators. The questionaires were sent to a stratified sample of three school districts in northern California. District A received 100 questionnaires and returned 79 (79 percent). District B received 25 questionnaires and returned 22 (88 percent). District C received 25 questionnaires and returned 23 (92 percent). A total of 124 questionnaires (82 percent) were returned, 69 by teacher aides, 43 by teachers, and 12 by administrators. The interpretations of the study were based on 124 questionnaires.

RESEARCH INSTRUMENT

The questionnaire, *Survey of Perceptions of Bilingual-Bicultural Instructional Aide Functions,* was developed delineating the functions in five major areas: Instructional, Bilingual-Bicultural, Clerical and Monitorial, Professional Development, and School-Community Liaison functions.

RESULTS OF THE STUDY

The results of the study are based on analysis of the ten null hypotheses tested. The data are presented within each hypothesis. They are discussed under five categories of functions designed for this study. The categories were: (1) Bilingual-Bicultural, (2) Instructional, (3) Professional Development, (4) School-Community Liaison, and (5) Clerical and Monitorial.

Hypotheses 1, 2, and 3 were designed to test for consensus among the groups regarding their perceptions of desirable instructional-aide functions, frequency of their occurrence, and competence of the aides' performance of desirable functions in the classroom. The findings of these hypotheses seemed to reveal that the groups knew ideally what the functions of the bilingual aides were and how often these aides were performing the functions, when the groups retained hypothesis 1 and 2 for 84 percent of the functions. However, closer interpretations of hypothesis 3 revealed that, although the groups knew ideally what the role of the bilingual aides was and how often they seemed to be performing the functions, the groups disagreed significantly in what they perceived to be the competence of the instructional aides in performing the functions. The main areas of disagreement were in the Bilingual-Bicultural and Instructional functions.

Hypotheses 4 through 9 were tested to look at the degree of consensus within each group regarding their perceptions of (1) assumed role functions and occurrence of these and (2) assumed role functions and effectiveness of role performance. Hypothesis 4 tested the first relationship for the teacher group. Significant differences were found in the perceptions of this group for thirty (38 percent) of the functions. Eighteen of these functions were in the Bilingual-Bicultural and Instructional categories.

Hypothesis 5 tested the perceptions of the administrator group. These findings indicated that the administrators saw few significant differences in the areas of desirability and frequency. The administrator group seemed to be closer in their perceptions regarding what they believed were the actual and the ideal role functions of the bilingual aides. The administrator group retained the hypothesis for 92 percent of the functions.

Hypothesis 6 tested the perceptions of the instructional-aide group regarding the same areas of desirability and frequency of role performance of the bilingual aides. This group yielded the highest degree of variability in what they perceived were desirable functions for the bilingual aides to perform and what they believed was actually taking place in the classroom. Hypothesis 6 was rejected for *every* function in the Bilingual-Bicultural category, sixteen functions in the Instructional category, eight functions in the Professional Development category, twelve functions in the School-Community Liaison category, and eleven functions in the Clerical and Monitorial category. The instructional aides rejected the hypothesis for sixty-eight (85 percent) of the functions.

The area of perceived competence of the bilingual-bicultural instructional aides in performing their functions was addressed by the results of hypotheses 3, 7, 8, and 9. This area yielded the largest significant differences in the perceptions of the groups. The Bilingual-Bicultural, Instructional, and Clerical and Monitorial categories were the main areas of disagreement.

The perceptions regarding the competence of role performance of the bilingual paraprofessionals among the groups were tested by hypothesis 3. The results indicated that there were twenty-one functions (25 percent) in which the three referent groups disagreed significantly. The hypothesis was rejected in those functions that required special skills with translations, direct pupil instruction using content areas, and evaluation of pupils' work with the assignment of grades. Closer interpretation of hypotheses 7 through 9 revealed specifically which groups seemed to disagree in certain areas.

The teacher group showed more concern in the area of perceived competence of role performance than the administrator group. This was indicated by the greater number of functions for which the hypotheses were rejected by each group. The teacher group rejected hypothesis 7 for twenty-one (25 percent) of the Bilingual-Bicultural functions. However, the administrator group rejected hypothesis 8 for only nine functions (11 percent) in the same combined areas. The instructional-aide group showed significant statistical differences in hypothesis 9. The group rejected the hypothesis for seventy-one (89 percent) of the functions. They rejected the hypothesis for *every* function in the Bilingual-Bicultural and Instructional categories. These results seemed to indicate that the bilingual-bicultural instructional aides knew what their role functions ideally should be but felt they were not competent to perform them.

Hypothesis 10 was included to test for any significant influences of biographical data on the perceived role functions. Significant differences were found in the perceptions of the groups for 19 percent of the functions. The groups' perceptions of desirable instructional-aide role functions seemed to be influenced by the age, sex, and instructional grade levels of the respondents. However, for 81 percent of the functions, biographical variables were not a significant influence on the perceptions of the groups regarding desirable instructional-aide functions.

In sum, the findings of the study indicate the following:

1. There were significant differences in the perceptions of the three referent groups regarding the role functions, frequency of occurrence of role functions, and perceived competence of role performance of the bilingual-bicultural instructional aides.

2. There were significant differences between what the groups perceived to be the ideal and actual role functions of the aides. The largest discrepancies in perceptions were indicated by the teacher and instructional-aide groups.

3. Most significant differences recorded by the groups were in the areas of Bilingual-Bicultural and Instructional functions.

4. The area of perceived competence of role performance showed the largest number of functions for which the hypotheses were rejected.

CONCLUSIONS

The conclusions of the researcher are based on the results of the study, which showed that there were significant differences among the teachers, administrators, and bilingual-bicultural instructional aides in what they perceived to be the ideal and actual role functions and the competence of the bilingual-bicultural instructional aides in the bilingual classrooms. When each group was polled separately, only the administrators saw these aides effectively performing their proper roles. Significant differences were found between teachers and administrators in what they perceived the aides should do and what they saw the aides actually doing. These groups also differed significantly in how they perceived the competence of the bilingual instructional aides. The instructional aides showed the largest degree of variability in their perceptions.

Several explanations for the discrepancies could be offered. The researcher submits that those involved with the hiring and placement of aides are seldom given adequate time to discuss and determine the role functions because of the immediate need of placing the bilingual-bicultural instructional aides in bilingual classrooms and because of the lack of proper interviews, training, and placement. There is seldom adequate time for proper training prior to the placement of the bilingual aides in the classroom.

The administrators appeared to be more in agreement in what they believed to be the role functions and the competencies of the bilingual-bicultural instructional aides. These findings could be attributed to the differences in sample size of the administrators (twelve) as compared to the sample size of the teachers (forty-three) and the instructional aides (sixty-nine). It also could be due to the fact that administrators had more experience educationally and in working and dealing with bilingual aides. On the other hand, although there were fewer functions for which significant differences were found in the perceptions of this group, the perceptions of the teacher and instructional-aide groups differed greatly.

The researcher concludes, therefore, that this could be due to the fact that administrators seldom work directly in the classroom with these aides. They do not seem to have the same opportunity to see what the aides do and how well they do it. They are more likely to take for granted what they feel should be taking place. The teachers could see what functions the instructional aides performed on a daily basis. They could evaluate the aides' competence based on their performance. In most cases, teachers are also responsible for the training of the bilingual aides. This gives them an additional opportunity to analyze their role functions and their competence in performing the functions.

From the results of hypotheses 1 and 2, it appeared that the groups had a fair indication of what the role functions of the instructional aides were and of how often the aides were performing the functions. However, closer interpretations of hypotheses 4 through 6 revealed that the aides were not really seen as performing the desired functions frequently. This was true especially in the Bilingual-Bicultural and Instructional areas. From these findings, one might conclude that the bilingual-bicultural instructional aides were not being utilized effectively in the specific areas for which they were being hired and trained. The groups also revealed that the bilingual aides were still performing more clerical duties than was perceived to be desired. These findings seemed to be consistent with those of Frank Morales, who stated that most duties being performed by bilingual aides were noninstructional and not related directly to bilingual education. The functions most frequently performed were clerical assignments.

All three groups perceived the competence of role performance of the bilingual paraprofessionals in a significantly different way. Again, the administrators seemed to show more consistency in what they perceived to be the competence of these aides in the bilingual classrooms. However, neither teachers nor instructional aides indicated that the aides were competent to perform most functions. Significant differences were found in their perceptions of all those functions that dealt with specific bilingual-bicultural and instructional skills. The groups seemed to feel that the instructional aides were especially incompetent in performing functions that dealt with translations of curriculum materials and translations dealing with parents or students.

These findings seemed to be consistent with those of Marilyn Seymann, who found that the bilingual aides were not competent to perform functions that dealt with translations, teaching methodology, and language instruction. The findings of the study seem to indicate that these differences in perceptions regarding the competence of the instructional aides were not attributed to the groups' lack of knowledge regarding the ideal role functions of the bilingual instructional aides as much as they seemed to be attributed to what they perceived to be lack of training. The researcher suggests that it could also have been due to a lack of confidence of the groups in the aides' abilities to perform the functions. Both teachers and aides seemed to have confidence in the abilities of the bilingual aides to perform functions not related to teaching nor to bilingual education. However, only the administrator group thought that the aides were competent to perform most bilingual-bicultural and instructional functions.

In sum, the conclusions of the researcher based on the study are as follows:

1. The role functions of the bilingual-bicultural instructional aides were perceived differently by the groups. The administrators seemed to show more consensus regarding the ideal functions. This was probably due to the fact that most administrators do not work directly with aides.

2. Lack of consensus regarding the actual role performance of these bilingual aides was apparently due to many factors. One of these factors could be the lack of communication among those directly involved with the interviewing, hiring, training, and placing of the aides.

3. While the administrators seemed to agree on the relationship between what the aides were doing in the classroom and how competent they were in performing their functions, this was not true for the teachers and the instructional aides. The aides agreed least about their role and seemed to show the least confidence in their abilities to perform their functions. This might be an indication again that the teachers and administrators were perhaps taking for granted certain strengths and weaknesses of the bilingual-bicultural instructional aides.

4. The bilingual-bicultural instructional aides were not performing the specific functions for which they were hired because apparently they were not competent. However, only the instructional aides seemed to feel that they were not receiving the appropriate training. Both teachers and administrators seemed to feel that the aides were adequately engaged in functions involving professional development.

RECOMMENDATIONS

In view of the above conclusions, the following recommendations are suggested for consideration:

1. Teachers, administrators, and working bilingual-bicultural instructional aides should prepare, prior to the interviewing and hiring of new aides, detailed job descriptions and selection criteria which outline the specific functions that the bilingual-bicultural instructional aides are to perform.

From these job descriptions, the interviewing committees can then determine the specific areas of competence the new candidates should have. At the time of the interviews, the specific strengths and weaknesses of the new aides could be noted so that conflicting expectations regarding their functions and competencies do not develop. Diagnostic training can then follow, based on the initial observations. Placement in the classrooms can also be based on these considerations.

Interviewers of bilingual-bicultural instructional aides should pay special attention to the language competencies of the applicants. This is especially important because in most cases the hiring of these aides will be based on oral interviews where they will appear to be bilingual-bicultural and where the interviewers are likely to conclude that they are, therefore, also biliterate. Screening should be conducted carefully to determine the applicants' performance in all four areas: speaking, writing, listening, and reading in the two languages that they are expected to utilize in the bilingual classroom.

2. Bilingual-bicultural instructional aides who demonstrate the need for language training should receive it as an essential and continuous part of their training. The following three areas of special concern for which colleges and teacher trainers can develop courses or training sessions are recommended:

a. Most aides will need to develop personal skills in speaking, writing, reading, and listening for the areas of content instruction. It is especially important that they take courses taught in the target language(s) in which they are expected to teach. It may not help to take courses in English about "Matematica bilingüe," for example. The aides will need to develop both the teaching methodology and content vocabularies in the target language(s).

b. Most aides will need to develop specific skills on how to translate instructional materials. This would be especially important in mathematics, science, and social studies. A course in techniques of translation would be valuable, and it is needed due to lack of skills of the bilingual aides, lack of bilingual materials, and the need to translate existing materials. This is an area that has been taken for granted and that is sorely needed today.

c. Courses or training sessions that provide second language instruction (ESL) should continue to be taught with emphasis on the immediate needs of the language-minority children, the limited skills of the bilingual instructional aides, and time and monies available for the training.

3. Training types of activities such as preservices, in-services, workshops, and college courses should be conducted for "teams" made up of teacher and aide or teacher-aide-administrator. This type of training is essential so that those working with the bilingual instructional aides will not develop conflicting expectations for the aides' role functions and competencies.

a. Courses in team-teaching techniques should be developed for "bilingual" teaching teams. These courses should emphasize the role of each member of the team, the utilization of each member's strengths, the improvement of each member's weaknesses, and the utilization of the bilingual-bicultural skills of each member of the team.

b. Curriculum-development training courses should be instituted for teams of teachers and aides. Here the knowledge and experience of the professional in teaching methodology can be utilized to develop needed materials and at the same time train the bilingual aides. In turn, the bilingual-bicultural skills of the bilingual aides can be utilized to train the monolingual professional. The bilingual curriculum that is developed in these courses should have immediate utility in the bilingual classroom.

c. Once the bilingual-bicultural instructional aides are placed in the classroom, continuous training and close supervision are essential. Team planning time should be regularly scheduled for teachers and their aides in order to constantly review, reinforce, and evaluate the strengths and weaknesses of each member of the team.

4. Teachers working with bilingual-bicultural instructional aides need and should have specific training in order to learn how best to utilize the skills of the bilingual paraprofessionals. Courses and training in the area of special pedagogical skills would also help teachers meet the criteria for bilingual-teacher competencies recommended by the California State Department of Education (1977) and seconded by this researcher. The bilingual teacher should have—

a. ability to identify the role and functions of each member of the instructional team (paraprofessionals);

    b. knowledge of the theoretical and practical aspects of team teaching and other organizational structures;

    c. skills in planning instructional activities with and for each member of the bilingual classroom team;

    d. the ability to use management skills, including the utilization of paraprofessionals;

    e. skills in specific instructional techniques in bilingual teaching. Major content areas include . . . team teaching. (pp. 18-19)

Monolingual teachers working with bilingual-bicultural instructional aides should have courses that will help them identify the uniqueness of the second language and culture of the aides. Teachers need to understand how the minority culture manifests itself in the behavior and learning styles of both teacher aides and students. This is needed so that the curriculum, instructional techniques, and materials selected and used will best meet not only the needs of the students but also the skills of the aides.

5. Administrators should be more actively involved in all phases of interviewing, hiring, training, placement, and evaluation of the bilingual-bicultural instructional aides.

This is essential so that conflicting expectations of the bilingual aides' responsibilities, competencies, and contributions to the bilingual classrooms do not develop. This researcher recommends that the administrators take more time and effort for the professional development of their bilingual aides in order to insure that the skills of these aides are being utilized and developed properly. The professional development of the bilingual-bicultural instructional aides should not be left up to the teachers and outside consultants only. The administrators of bilingual programs should also have the responsibilities of training the bilingual aides in specific areas that need the coordinating skills of the administrators. In many cases, only the administrators would be able to describe the specific needs of a school site. It would be of great benefit to have the administrators train the teachers and instructional aides in such cases. Improved communications among teachers, administrators, and bilingual aides would also develop in this way.

The need for bilingual-bicultural instructional aides to serve in bilingual programs is recognized today. Their lack of adequate training to perform their functions is also recognized. Questions of how best to train these aides and maximize their contributions in the classroom are always voiced, but little is ever said about the need to recognize their contributions. This researcher, as part of a final recommendation, suggests that the bilingual paraprofessionals must be given credit and recognition for their contributions to bilingual programs. Teachers and administrators must begin to see the bilingual-bicultural instructional aides as part of the teaching teams and not just as temporary helpers. Respect for the educational and personal needs of these aides has to exist before a "team spirit" can be expected to occur. The aides must receive respect in the form of educational advantages and training, and they must be accepted by teachers and administrators as a part of the team. The attainment of a much deserved recognition of the aides' contributions to bilingual programs can contribute significantly toward helping them to achieve their maximum potential. In this manner, bilingual-bicultural educators can more effectively work together toward meeting the needs of all students.

Recommendations for Further Study

1. The review of the educational literature and the results of this study have pointed out that there are significant differences in the perceptions of teachers, administrators, and instructional aides regarding the role of bilingual-bicultural instructional aides. The results of this study could have been attributed to many factors. One of the factors could have been the size of the sample and the differences in size of the three referent groups and school districts. Similar studies, then, should be conducted which use larger samples and equal-size referent groups and school-district samples.

2. This study has contributed to the development of job descriptions based upon the consensus of three referent groups. A further study should be conducted to test the validity of these job descriptions in terms of their relationship to the classroom effectiveness of bilingual-bicultural instructional aides.

3. The review of the literature also revealed that few studies have been conducted which were designed to evaluate the contributions of bilingual-bicultural instructional aides toward the academic achievement of language-minority students. These few studies can only point to the indirect ways whereby the use of bilingual paraprofessionals has helped improve academic achievement. It is evident that there is a need for studies to investigate the direct effects of bilingual-bicultural instructional aides on the academic progress of language-minority children.

4. In order to facilitate effective studies and to improve the validity of further investigations in this area, concerted efforts should be made to develop appropriate research techniques and instruments.

APPENDIX
Sample Questionnaire

Survey of Perceptions of Bilingual-Bicultural Instructional Aide Functions

Instructions: Please mark *one choice for each side* which comes nearest to your perceptions of the (1) functions, (2) frequency of occurrence of these, and (3) competency in these functions for the bilingual-bicultural instructional aide in the bilingual-bicultural classroom. If you have any questions on how to proceed, please ask.

The instructional aide:	(1) Do you believe this should occur?					(2) How frequently do you believe this occurs?				(3) In general, how competent do you believe aides are?				
	Strongly Disagree	Disagree	Undecided	Agree	Strongly Agree	Always	Often	Seldom	Never	Highly Competent	Competent	Somewhat Competent	Not Competent, Need Training	
1. Interprets attendance laws and other school regulations to non-English-speaking parents.														
2. Instructs small groups of students in various language-arts areas.														
3. Performs errands outside school grounds during working hours.														
4. Attends curriculum meetings.														
5. Arranges for presentations of cultural arts and crafts, food, music, etc.														
6. Presents and reads children's literature to students.														
7. Develops a close relationship between school and neighborhood attendance area.														
8. Takes roll call and maintains other official school records for students.														

REFERENCES

Assembly Bill No. 1329, Chapter 5.76. Bilingual-Bicultural Education Act of 1976.

Barba, A. M. A. "New Mexico Project Aides: Perceptions of Their Functions." Ph.D. dissertation, New Mexico State University, 1973.

Barnard, Chester I. *The Functions of the Executive.* Cambridge, Mass: Harvard University Press, 1966.

Bowman, Garda W., and Klopf, Gordon J. *New Careers and Roles in the American School.* New York: Bank Street College of Education, for the Office of Economic Opportunity, 1968.

Getzels, Jacob W. "Conflict and Role Behavior in the Educational Setting." *Readings in the Social Psychology of Education,* edited by W. W. Charters and N. C. Gage, pp. 311–16. Boston: Allyn and Bacon, Inc., 1964.

Godwin, Douglas G. "The Bilingual Teacher Aide: Classroom Asset." *The Elementary School Journal* 77 (March 1977).

Isaac, Stephen, and Michael, William B. *Handbook in Research and Education.* San Diego, Calif.: Robert R. Knapp, Publisher, 1974.

Leighton, E. Roby. *Proceedings of the Conference on the Use and Roles of Teacher Aides.* U.S., Educational Resources Information Center, ERIC ED 031 436, 1969.

Morales, Frank J. "A Descriptive Study of Bilingual Teacher Aides and Their Utilization in Elementary Spanish-English Bilingual Classrooms." Ph.D. dissertation, University of New Mexico, 1976.

Ollio, P. A. "Perceptions of the Roles of Teacher Aides as Reported by Selected Principals, Teachers, and Teacher Aides in Dade County, Florida." Ph.D. dissertation, University of Miami, 1971.

Sarbin, Theodore R. "Role Theory." *Handbook of Social Psychology,* edited by Gardner Lindzey. Reading, Mass.: Addison-Wesley, 1954.

Seymann, Marilyn R. *Research and Analysis of Competencies Needed by the Bilingual Teacher Aide.* Mesa, Arizona: Mesa Community College, 1976.

State Department of Education. "Criteria for Bilingual Teacher Competencies." Draft presented by the committee to set criteria for California's bilingual-teacher competencies, pp. 18-19. Sacramento, Calif.: July 1977.

Tollett, Charles, and Tollett, Dan. "Teacher Aide Laws Invite Lawsuits against Schools." *The American School Board Journal* 161 (July 1974).

U.S., Commission on Civil Rights. *A Better Chance to Learn: Bilingual Bicultural Education.* Publication No. 51. Washington, D.C.: May 1975.

Zalk, Kenda, et al. *The Role of the Paraprofessional in Bilingual Education.* U.S., Educational Resources Information Center, ERIC ED 132 218, 1975.

A Sociolinguistic Study of Crow Language Maintenance

John A. S. Read

Semifinalist, Outstanding Dissertations
National Advisory Council on Bilingual Education

Degree conferred August 1978
University of New Mexico
Albuquerque, New Mexico

Dissertation Committee:
Bernard Spolsky, *Chair*
Vera John-Steiner
Alan Hudson-Edwards
Leroy Ortiz

About the Author

Dr. John A. S. Read is currently working at the Regional Language Center in Singapore.

ABSTRACT

This is an investigation of the extent to which the Crow Indian Tribe of Montana has maintained its own language rather than shifting completely to English. Sociolinguistic surveys of both adult tribal members and Crow schoolchildren revealed a high level of language maintenance at all age levels. Then an extensive analysis was undertaken of the tribe's historical relations with American society and its present sociocultural situation, in order to understand the foundations of its language maintenance and provide a sociolinguistic perspective on the planning of bilingual programs in Crow reservation schools. It was concluded that the Crow were a cohesive group who had adapted pragmatically to modern life while retaining the core of their tribal culture, of which the language was an indispensable element. In sociolinguistic terms, the need for bilingual education was obvious, but its development was constrained by problems related to teacher training, funding, school administration, and Crow literacy.

STATEMENT OF THE PROBLEM

This dissertation comprises a study of the degree of language maintenance among the Crow Tribe of Indians in southeastern Montana, including an analysis of how the language is maintained and a discussion of what this means for bilingual education on the Crow reservation. For the purposes of this study, language maintenance was defined as a situation where an ethnic minority group has a bilingual repertoire composed of its own language and the dominant language of the society, with a stable pattern of usage in which each language is associated with particular social functions.

In the United States, the long-term prospect for minority-group languages is generally presumed to be not language maintenance but language shift, a process of declining proficiency in and usage of the ethnic language leading eventually to its complete displacement by English. That this generalization applies to American Indian languages is indicated by the results of the one comprehensive survey of their numbers of speakers by Chafe (1962), who found that 40 percent of the languages had fewer than a hundred speakers and 60 percent were not normally spoken by anyone under twenty years of age. However, until recently very little research has been undertaken on the process of shift, either in general or among individual tribes. Not much is known about the pattern of language use in Indian communities or the nonlinguistic factors that contribute to language maintenance or bring about language shift.

With the passage of the federal Bilingual Education Act came a practical reason for studies of language maintenance: to establish the need for bilingual instruction and to assist in planning the implementation of it. As a result, some significant studies have been made of the sociolinguistic situation of the Crow and Northern Cheyenne (Dracon 1970), the Navajo (Spolsky 1974), and the Oklahoma Cherokee (Guyette 1976). In the Crow case, Dracon reported that 82 percent of Crow students at all grade levels were primary speakers of their tribal language, a remarkably high percentage. The goal of the present dissertation, then, was to confirm Dracon's findings longitudinally and to extend them through a survey of adult language usage and an investigation of the sociocultural foundations upon which such strong language maintenance might be based. The research was undertaken in conjunction with an educational needs assessment by the tribe's Central Education Commission and was intended to produce a resource document that could be used in program planning and bilingual teacher training for reservation schools.

In short, the dissertation is divided into three main sections: the report of the surveys on the extent of Crow maintenance among adults and children; the analysis of the nonlinguistic variables contributing to the strength of the language maintenance; and the discussion of the educational implications of the study.

SOCIOLINGUISTIC SURVEYS

Adult Language Usage

In the case of the sociolinguistic surveys, separate studies were undertaken of adults and children. Data on adult language usage and attitudes were gathered by means of an interview schedule that was administered to an 18-percent sample of Crow family heads as part of a comprehensive socioeconomic survey of the tribe conducted by a special tribal research unit. The schedule comprised seven multipart questions concerning the respondents' relative use of Crow and English in various situations, their preferences in language choice, their attitudes towards the present and future roles of each language, and their assessment of the importance of Crow in relation to other elements of their culture.

As expected, the results revealed a high level of Crow language use. Only 10 percent of the respondents reported being brought up as monolingual speakers of English. Conversely, 72 percent of them used Crow always or mostly in conversation with another Crow speaker. Even in situations where English might have been expected to predominate, Crow was the main medium of communication. For example, only 18 percent of the subjects always used English in their work, and in discussing proposed coal-mining developments on the reservation, 76 percent of them used Crow at least half the time. The evidence indicated that the single most important variable determining language choice was whether the interlocutor spoke Crow, rather than the setting or the topic of conversation. Despite the predominant use of Crow, when the respondents were asked to state their preference rather than their actual usage, there was a strong tendency for them to prefer that both languages be spoken in public and be taught at home and school.

On questions concerning the present state and the future of Crow, there were few strong opinions, except that 89 percent of the subjects disagreed that Crow should be completely displaced by English. The continuing maintenance of Crow appeared to be taken for granted. The respondents were generally pragmatic in their acceptance of the widespread use of English loans in Crow speech and in their lack of objection to the learning of Crow by non-Indians. On the other hand, they ranked the language as one of the three most important elements of their culture, both in its own right and as a vehicle for the expression of kinship relations, religious beliefs, ancestral tales, and ritual observances.

With regard to their children's language education, the respondents recognized the importance of English as the dominant medium of instruction. A large plurality of them (44 percent) preferred that both languages be taught in the home; almost as many (39 percent) justified the use of English at home as a means of improving their children's school achievement. In addition, they reported actually speaking considerably more English to their children than to their contemporaries. On the other hand, half of those interviewed wanted both languages to be taught in school, and 57 percent considered it desirable for non-Crow-speaking children to have the opportunity to learn the language at school. Only 15 percent believed that teachers should try to stop children from speaking Crow in school. Thus, although the adults were disposed to make concessions to English for educational purposes, they also envisaged a significant role for their own hitherto excluded language in the education system.

Language Proficiency in Reservation Schools

The second survey was a study of the language proficiency of Crow students in reservation schools. From the adult survey, there were some indications that language shift might be in progress among the younger generation, given the importance attached by respondents to the learning of English by their children. On the other hand, the 1969 data gathered by Dracon (1970) had shown a uniformly high percentage of dominant Crow speakers at all grade levels in the schools.

Although the present survey was designed to be comparable with that of Dracon, it was not strictly a duplication since the rating system and procedure were modified to some degree. For rating purposes, the following categories were adopted:

Cϕ = speaks only Crow
Ce = speaks Crow and a limited amount of English
CE = speaks Crow and English with equal ability
cE = speaks English and a limited amount of Crow
ϕE = speaks only English

In order to be able to test the validity of the results, two rating procedures were used. First, two residents from each of the reservation communities were selected to learn the rating system and rate all the students in their local schools, on the assumption that the apparently comprehensive acquaintance that Crow people have with other Crow families would allow them to assess the children's language abilities quite accurately. Then, secondly, a random sample of 20 percent of the students was selected to be rated on the basis of a short interview conducted by a bilingual Crow who had not been involved with the community ratings.

Comparison of the results from the two ratings revealed considerable differences in the distribution of the students among rating categories. However, both sets of ratings classified 73 percent of the students as Cϕ, Ce, or CE, meaning that they were primary speakers of Crow. This was about 9 percent lower than the figure of 82 percent reported by Dracon (1970), but given the differences in procedure and the imprecision inherent in this kind of survey, it is debatable whether an actual decline in language maintenance had occurred from 1969 to 1976. As was the case in 1969, no significant difference was found between the upper and lower grades in their level of Crow maintenance.

With regard to the question of validity, a comparison was made of the two ratings given to the students in the interview sample, who were rated both by the community raters and by the interviewer. In 70 percent of the cases, the two ratings coincided; 96 percent of them differed by no more than one point on the rating scale. Most of the discrepancies could readily be explained in terms of the different procedures involved in the two ratings and slight differences in the interpretation of the categories. It appeared then that, given the limitations of this kind of survey, there was a high degree of validity in the judgments of the community raters.

ANALYSIS OF NONLINGUISTIC VARIABLES

Once the present level and scope of Crow language maintenance had been established by the two surveys, the second major phase of the research was an analysis of the sociocultural situation of the tribe, in order to seek an understanding of the nonlinguistic factors contributing to the maintenance of the language. To begin this analysis, a review was made of the literature on language maintenance and bilingualism, with particular reference to American Indian tribes. The review led to the identification of a number of nonlinguistic variables, which may be summarized briefly.

Assuming that the object of study is a minority ethnic group with its own distinctive language, we need to consider various aspects of the group's situation. First there is its isolation—both geographical and social—from speakers of other languages, which is related to rural versus urban residence. It also appears to make a difference whether the group is indigenous to the territory or immigrant in origin. Internally, significant factors are the size of the group, its cohesiveness, and its self-sufficiency. Cohesion is reflected in the strength of the religious, cultural, and economic bonds between group members; the prospects for language maintenance are apparently enhanced if the ethnic language is regarded as the indispensable means of expression for those bonds. Self-sufficiency tends to be associated with rural isolation, but it is also a function of group size and the group's ability to maintain its own social institutions, notably (for our purposes) its own schools.

Of equal importance is the nature of the relations between the group and the wider society. The group's resolve to preserve its traditions may be stiffened by forcible efforts to acculturate the group members and to suppress their language, whereas their assimilation into the mainstream of society can be facilitated by positive attitudes towards them and by compatibility between the two cultures. One particularly salient indicator of the state of intergroup relations is the incidence of intermarriage. Another factor, which may be inversely related to group cohesion, is the desire of minority-group members to participate in the majority society. People are more likely to want to enter the mainstream if their ethnic community has disintegrated or if they as migrants have lost their links with the community.

Given the number of variables that may influence language maintenance, there was a need for a theoretical framework within which they could be discussed in a systematic manner. For the present study, the theory employed was the framework of comparative ethnic relations developed by Schermerhorn (1970). The applicability of this theory to sociolinguistic research had been recognized by several scholars, including Paulston (1975), who used it to interpret apparently contradictory data from bilingual education programs in various parts of North America. Fundamentally the theory seeks to identify the conditions that facilitate or hinder the integration of subordinate (nonmainstream) ethnic groups into the society at large. It comprises three independent and three dependent variables whose definitions are set out in the appendix. The dissertation includes an extensive discussion of each variable and its relevance to the study of language maintenance.

It is the first and second independent variables of the framework that provide the key to understanding the Crow situation. The first one focuses on the historical sequence of interaction between the ethnic group and the dominant society. Thus a survey was made of the evolution of relations between the Crow tribe and Anglo-American society from the early nineteenth century to the present time. It was concluded from the historical evidence that the Crow are an indigenous, colonized people who have remained on a desirable portion of their prereservation territory. While they did not welcome the changes wrought by the westward expansion of the United States, they foresaw the inevitability of the process and sought to accommodate themselves to it as best they could. Despite their consistently friendly relations with the Americans, they suffered most of the same indignities and privation as other tribes did during the transition to reservation life. Later, paternalistic government administration and missionary activity was followed by what was in effect the opening of the reservation to settlement by non-Indian ranching families, whose presence is still an important factor complicating the status of the reservation as an Indian enclave. Thus, the Crow have been subjected to great pressures to relinquish both their land and their way of life; they have not resisted inflexibly but in a pragmatic fashion have adapted to their changed circumstances while retaining an essential core of their culture, of which the most obvious manifestation is the language.

The other key variable in the Schermerhorn framework is the degree of enclosure of the ethnic group, defined as the extent to which the group maintains its own social institutions separate from those of the mainstream society. In these terms, the Crow were found to be enclosed to a significant degree from their non-Indian neighbors. Intermarriage is a recent phenomenon and usually involves non-Crows from off the reservation. Kinship bonds are strong, being expressed informally through the structure of the extended family and formally by the practice of the clan system. It follows that patterns of friendship and recreational activities also tend to be ethnically enclosed. While Crows participate in both Indian and non-Indian forms of religion, in the latter case they generally worship separately from non-Indian members of the same denomination. The schools are one setting where the two groups come together in a single institution, but in various ways the ethnic barriers that exist elsewhere are preserved there. Until the past decade, the school has been very much a non-Indian domain—as shown by the composition of its governing board, faculty, student body, and curricula—and Crow parents and children have not participated on an equal basis. Politically the tribe has constitutional status and a measure of self-government, although there are recurring legal challenges by non-Indians to the concept of tribal sovereignty and the tribe is increasingly subject to the actions of various external governmental authorities. There is an economic basis for survival on the reservation, especially from federal welfare programs and leasing of the land, with the prospect of considerable prosperity if the coal reserves are fully exploited. In sum, then, the Crow have maintained a significant degree of enclosure from the English speakers and the English-medium institutions that surround them, creating a social environment in which Crow can continue as the major means of communication.

EDUCATIONAL IMPLICATIONS

The third and final section of the dissertation presents a discussion of the educational implications of Crow language maintenance. First, the research showed that there was a high degree of Crow maintenance throughout the tribe and, in particular, at all grade levels in the schools. This is important because maintenance of an Indian language among the younger generation cannot be assumed, even if the language is widely spoken in the adult population. A relatively rapid shift to English can occur from one generation to the next, and there is a fundamental difference in approach between a program that builds on the Indian-language proficiency that the students already have and one that sets out to revive the language among children who have largely lost it. The maintenance of Crow is such that the former approach is appropriate in Crow reservation schools.

Secondly, it was found that there was considerable support among Crow adults for the use of Crow in the schools. The Crow generally had pride in their language and did not consider it unworthy of being a medium of instruction. Further, there was apparently no inclination to keep the language out of the education system for fear that non-Indians might gain access to the enclosed realm of the traditional culture and religion. This does not necessarily mean, though, that Crow as a Second Language for non-Indian students could become an important component of Crow bilingual programs. One needs to take into account the tensions between Crows and non-Indians on the reservation and the degree of enclosure separating them, in spite of the fact that their children have been educated in the same schools for nearly sixty years. Related to this is the question of who controls the schools. Crow reservation schools have been administered by non-Indian school boards until recently, when changing demographic patterns and the availability of federal education funds have given Crows more influence in the schools and created a more favorable climate for bilingual education.

Another important matter that is discussed is literacy in Crow, on the assumption that the role of a language in formal education is limited unless the students are literate in it and have adequate reading materials. It is reported that Crow remains almost entirely an oral medium of communication, in spite of efforts in the last decade to develop a writing system, produce reading matter, and promote literacy in the language. Little indication was found that Crow literacy would have any significant role in the linguistic repertoire of Crow adults in the future, and this is seen as limiting the prospects for Crow as a medium of instruction in the schools beyond the primary grades.

One further topic is the training of Crow bilingual teachers and the question of how they can be most effectively employed in the classrooms. Various ways in which the classroom might reflect the sociolinguistic patterns of interaction among Crows are discussed. It was concluded that the most enduring legacy of bilingual education on the reservation may be a corps of certified Crow teachers who could shape a truly bilingual and bicultural education system for the tribe.

APPENDIX
The Schermerhorn Framework of Comparative Ethnic Relations

Integration of ethnic groups into a society is proposed as a composite function of three independent and three intervening variables. The independent variables posited here are:

I. (1) repeatable sequences of interaction between subordinate ethnics and dominant groups, such as annexation, migration, and colonization;

   (2) the degree of enclosure (institutional separation or segmentation) of the subordinate group or groups from the society-wide network of institutions and associations;

   (3) the degree of control exercised by dominant groups over access to scarce resources by subordinate groups in a given society.

The intervening or contextual variables that modify the effects of independent variables are:

II. (1) agreement or disagreement between dominant and subordinate groups on collective goals for the latter, such as assimilation and pluralism;

   (2) membership of a society under scrutiny in a class or category of societies sharing overall common cultural and structural features, such as Near East societies and Sub-Saharan societies;

   (3) membership of a society under scrutiny in a more limited category of societies distinguished by forms of institutional dominance, i.e., polity dominating economy or vice versa.

(Schermerhorn 1970, p. 15)

REFERENCES

Chafe, Wallace L. "Estimates Regarding the Present Speakers of North American Indian Languages." *International Journal of American Linguistics* 28 (1962): 162-71.

Dracon, John. *The Extent of Bilingualism among the Crow and the Northern Cheyenne Indian School Population, Grades One through Twelve—A Study.* ERIC ED 044 205, 1970.

Guyette, Susan M. "Sociolinguistic Determinants of Native Language Vitality: A Comparative Study of Two Oklahoma Cherokee Communities." Ph.D. dissertation, Southern Methodist University, 1976.

Paulston, Christina Bratt. "Ethnic Relations and Bilingual Education: Accounting for Contradictory Data." *Working Papers on Bilingualism*, no. 6 (May 1975), pp. 1-44.

Schermerhorn, R. A. *Comparative Ethnic Relations: A Framework for Theory and Research.* New York: Random House, 1970.

Spolsky, Bernard. "Speech Communities and Schools." *TESOL Quarterly* 8 (1974): 17-26.

A Comparative Study of Two Approaches of Introducing Initial Reading to Navajo Children: The Direct Method and the Native-Language Method

Paul Rosier

Semifinalist, Outstanding Dissertations
National Advisory Council on Bilingual Education

Degree conferred May 1977
Northern Arizona University
Flagstaff, Arizona

Dissertation Committee:
David Whorton, *Chair*
Paul Lansing
Sam Bliss
Haskell Cannon
Guy Bensuzan

About the Author

Dr. Paul Rosier has worked extensively in Navajo bilingual education. Dr. Rosier is currently the assistant principal at Page High School in Page, Arizona. In the past, he has served as the bilingual education coordinator at Rock Point Community School and the associate director of the Native American Materials Development Center. Dr. Rosier has published several articles and presented papers at a variety of conferences on bilingual education.

ABSTRACT

This study was a comparison of two approaches for introducing reading to Navajo children of limited English-speaking ability. The Direct Method approach introduced children to reading in English only. Systematic English as a Second Language techniques were used in this approach. The Native Language Method approach introduced children to initial reading in Navajo first. The children developed reading proficiency in the native language and later, at the second-grade level, the children were transferred to English reading. These children developed oral proficiency in English while they were learning to read in Navajo.

Data was collected over a three-year period. The results of the study were:

1. At the second-grade level, the Direct Method group achievement was generally higher than the Native Language Method group. The Direct Method mean scores were significantly higher in six of twenty T-test analyses.
2. At the third-grade level, the Native Language Method group achievement generally was equal to or greater than the Direct Method group achievement. The experimental group means were significantly higher in six of twenty analyses.
3. At the fourth-grade level, the Native Language Method group scores generally were higher than the Direct Method group scores. The Native Language Method group means were significantly higher in fifteen of twenty analyses.
4. At the fifth- and sixth-grade levels, the Native Language Method group mean scores were significantly higher than the Direct Method group mean scores in all analyses conducted.

OVERVIEW

The American educational system is designed for children whose native language is English. When confronted with children who speak only limited English, this system has not met their educational needs adequately. This is the situation in which Navajo Indian children find themselves.

Spolsky and Holm (1971) report the linguistic composition of Navajo six-year-olds entering school as follows:

> Overall, 73% of Navajo six-year-olds in the study (virtually complete for BIA schools, and including several of the largest public school systems) come to school not speaking enough English to do first grade work. . . . in Bureau schools less than 1% of the children are English monolinguals and

less than 3% are English dominant. Even in public schools less than 10% of the children are English monolinguals and less than 20% are English dominant (Spolsky and Holm 1971, p. 8).

The primary approach to teaching English for almost a hundred years was to prohibit children from using the Navajo language, i.e., children were punished if "caught" speaking Navajo at school. During the early sixties, a systematic-structural approach for teaching English to Navajo children was introduced on the reservation. Teaching English as a Second Language (TESL) methods were introduced in several Bureau of Indian Affairs (BIA) schools between 1960 and 1964. The results were so impressive that the BIA mandated the use of TESL programs in all their schools. During the late sixties and early seventies, public schools began to implement TESL programs.

Although the results of TESL methods improved student achievement, the 1972 Navajo Area BIA Stanford Achievement Test results revealed that children were still far below the national norms. The achievement scores released by the Navajo Area Education Office appear in Table 1 ("The Stanford Achievement . . . 1972," pp. 2-7).

The BIA's response to the above-mentioned results was to develop several TESL programs specifically for Navajo children. These programs have been refined and organized into two curricula approaches that are presently used by the BIA. Consultants In Total Education (CITE) and The Navajo Area Language Arts Program (NALAP) are used in most of the BIA schools on the Navajo reservation in grades 1-3.

The methods mentioned to this point are all monolingual English, Direct Method approaches. In the late sixties an alternative approach was introduced. This approach incorporated the TESL methods as one component and used the native language as another component, thus forming a bilingual approach.

Since this study focuses on reading, a brief description of the basic approach for each method of teaching reading will be presented. The Direct Method approach introduces the child to English using oral-aural techniques. After sufficient proficiency in English has been developed, usually after the first year, English reading is introduced. TESL techniques are used to teach reading, i.e., the vocabulary and syntactical structure are controlled. Ideally, the TESL oral-language program and the TESL controlled-reading techniques would be used until the child becomes a proficient speaker and reader of English.

Table 1
A Comparison of Navajo Student Average Achievement Scores and the National Norm on the Paragraph Meaning Subtests of the Stanford Achievement Test, 1972.

Grade Level	National Norm	Average Grade-Level Equivalent for Navajo Students	Difference Minus Plan
Second	2.5 [a]	1.8	.7
Third	3.5	2.4	1.1
Fourth	4.5	2.7	1.8
Fifth	5.5	3.6	1.9
Sixth	6.5	4.1	2.4

[a]The National Norm is determined by the date of the administration of the test. The test was administered in February 1972.

A bilingual or Native Language Method introduces reading in the native language first. After the child becomes a proficient reader in the native language, at the second or third-grade level, (s)he begins English reading. Most of the essential concepts of reading should transfer to English reading, i.e., that the printed page is an extension of language. During the time (s)he is learning to read in the native language, the child receives TESL instruction. The Native Language Method allows the child to learn to read in the language (s)he understands while (s)he is developing a proficiency in oral English.

In summary, both approaches are designed to help the child become a competent speaker of English. Both have as one of their goals the development of proficiency in reading English.

STATEMENT OF THE PROBLEM

This study was a comparison of two approaches (the Direct Method and the Native Language Method) of introducing Navajo children to initial reading of English. In one approach, the Direct Method, children (the control group) were introduced to reading in English only. In the other approach, the Native Language Method, children (the experimental group) were introduced to reading in Navajo first. The purpose of this study was to determine the effects of each of these two approaches on English-reading ability.

Hypotheses

Hypothesis 1. There will be no significant differences between the experimental group and the control group in total reading achievement at each grade level, second through sixth.

Hypothesis 2. There will be no significant differences between the experimental group and the control group in selected subskill areas—word knowledge or word-study skills and reading comprehension—at each grade level, second through sixth.

Hypothesis 3. There will be no difference between the experimental group and the control group in overall growth rate (grades second through sixth) in total reading achievement measured in grade-level-equivalent scores.

SIGNIFICANCE OF THE STUDY

Within the United States there are millions of children who speak no English or who speak only limited English. In the Supreme Court decision in the case of *Lau* v. *Nichols*, the court has ruled that a regular (standard American) school curriculum does not meet the specific needs of children of limited English-speaking ability (U.S. Commission on Civil Rights 1975, p. 179). Consequently, school districts will have to organize programs that will meet these needs. The basic decision faced by most districts is whether to implement a bilingual or direct TESL approach.

The Civil Rights Commission reports that more than 117 million dollars were expended for bilingual education by the federal government between 1969 and 1973 (U.S. Commission on Civil Rights, p. 171). Eighty million dollars were appropriated in fiscal year 1975 and 98 million dollars were appropriated for fiscal year 1976. In addition, many states are appropriating monies for bilingual education. The outlook for the near future is that considerably more money will be expended for bilingual education.

The results of this study could be applied to the above situations, but the primary purpose of this investigation was to provide information for Navajo parents and educators of Navajo children. The Navajo Tribe Division of Education estimates that there are 60,000 Navajo children in school on or near the reservation. The number is increasing annually (Division of Education 1973, p. 48). These children receive less than an equal education in English basic skills, as shown by the information in table 1. This study can provide information that may assist educational planners to provide a better educational foundation for these children.

Definition of Terms

- *Direct Method* is a monolingual English approach to reading, using English as a Second Language (ESL) techniques.

- *Native Language Method* is a bilingual approach to reading. Children first are introduced to reading in the native language and then transfer to English reading.
- *Experimental group* refers to children who are introduced to initial reading in the native language and later are transferred to English reading.
- *Baseline control group* refers to children who are introduced to initial reading in English only and are tested only once to establish baseline data.
- *Concurrent control group* refers to children who are introduced to initial reading in English only, but will be tested concurrently with the experimental group.
- *Index of language dominance* is a three-digit index numeral which indicates the degree of language dominance of six-year-olds entering a particular school (Spolsky 1971, p. 7).

METHODOLOGY

Introduction

The design of the study was structured after the Post-Test-Only Control Group Design model described by Campbell and Stanley (1966, pp. 25-27). This model was modified to meet existing conditions. Two divergences from the model were required: first, the participating schools were selected based on curricular criteria and were not randomly selected; second, two control groups were used rather than one. The two groups are referred to as the baseline control group and the concurrent control group.

Population and Sampling

The experimental and control schools were selected on curricular criteria. There was only one school serving Navajo children that had developed a bilingual program to the extent that the children had become proficient readers in Navajo before beginning English reading. Thus, the experimental group was limited to that school—Rock Point Community School.

The two control groups included selected samples of students in Bureau of Indian Affairs (BIA) schools on the Navajo reservation which use the Direct Method. Both control groups were composed of five schools. The schools for each control group were selected using the following criteria:

1. The schools had a program which included grades kindergarten through six.
2. The schools had an established CITE, NALAP, or other recognized TESL program.

3. There were two people per classroom involved in instruction in grades K-2.
4. At least one of the two instructors had native competence in Navajo.
5. The index of language dominance of entering six-year-olds for each school was within the limits of 3.48 to 5.00. Data were collected on entering six-year-olds in over 90 percent of the BIA schools and in more than 50 percent of the public schools on the Navajo reservation. From the data gathered, Spolsky developed a scale of language dominance and assigned each school an index number (Spolsky, pp. 7-15).

Data Collection

There were two comparisons in this study. The first compared the experimental group with the baseline control group. The control group in this case was tested in February 1975 to establish baseline data. The experimental group was also tested at that time and was tested again in February 1976 and February 1977. The instrument used in this comparison was the Stanford Achievement Test (SAT), 1973 edition. All administrations of the test were considered post-tests. Scores from three subtests were used. They included word-study skills, reading comprehension, and total reading.

The second comparison was between the experimental group and the concurrent control group. Both groups were tested over a one-year period. The BIA school system and Rock Point Community School both administered the Metropolitan Achievement Test (MAT) system wide in April, 1976. This administration was considered a posttest. All children in the control and experimental groups in the second through sixth grades were tested. Three scores were gathered—word knowledge, reading (comprehension), and total reading.

Statistical Analysis

Data were collected for each of the two comparisons: the experimental group and the baseline control group; the experimental group and the concurrent control group. Grade-level-equivalent scores of each student in the study were collected for: (1) each of the three test areas—word knowledge or word-study skills, reading comprehension, and total reading; (2) each grade level at each school; and (3) each year of the study.

The data gathered using the MAT were converted to SAT grade-level equivalents using a conversion table *(Stanford Research Report,*

1973, pp. 1-15). This conversion of MAT scores to SAT scores was completed before the data were analyzed statistically; consequently all data reported in this study are in the form of grade-level equivalents based on the Stanford Achievement Test, 1973 edition.

The data gathered for each of the two comparisons were independently analyzed. Also, the data collected each year of the study were analyzed separately. Comparisons between the years of the study and between the two sets of data were made, and significant trends are reported.

The data for both comparisons were statistically analyzed by use of a T-test. The T-test was used to analyze the difference of the means of each school and the means of the experimental group and each of the control groups. The .05 level of confidence was used as the criterion level for determining significant difference.

FINDINGS

The analysis of the data provides the following results. These results are expressed in general statements based on two separate comparisons, the baseline comparison and the concurrent comparison, and on data collected over a three-year period.

1. The comparisons conducted at the second-grade level revealed that the control-group achievement generally was higher than the experimental-group achievement. The control-group scores were significantly higher than the experimental-group scores in six of twenty comparisons made at the second-grade level.

2. The comparisons at the third-grade level showed that the experimental-group achievement generally was equal to or greater than the control-group achievement. The experimental-group means were significantly higher than the control-group means in six of twenty comparisons.

3. The comparisons of achievement at the fourth-grade level generally revealed that the experimental-group scores were higher than the control-group scores. The experimental-group means were significantly higher than the control-group means in fifteen of twenty comparisons.

4. The fifth-grade-level comparisons showed that the experimental-group means were significantly higher than the control-group means in all twenty comparisons.

5. The sixth-grade-level comparisons revealed that the experimental-group scores were significantly higher than the control-group scores in all fifteen comparisons.

Table 2
Summary of the Conclusions of the Hypotheses

Grade	Hypothesis 1 Total Reading	Hypothesis 2 Word Study	Hypothesis 2 Comprehension	Hypothesis 3 Girl/Girl	Hypothesis 3 Boy/Boy	Hypothesis 4
2	not rejected	not rejected	not rejected	not rejected	not rejected	—
3	not rejected	not rejected	not rejected	not rejected	not rejected	—
4	rejected	rejected	not rejected	rejected	rejected	—
5	rejected	rejected	rejected	rejected	rejected	—
6	rejected	rejected	rejected	rejected	rejected	—
OVERALL 2-6	—	—	—	—	—	rejected

CONCLUSIONS

A summary of the conclusions is presented in table 2. The table shows that at the second- and third-grade levels, none of the hypotheses 1-3 were rejected, but at the fourth-grade level, the hypotheses 1-3, except one component of hypothesis 2, were rejected. Hypotheses 1-3 were rejected at the fifth- and sixth-grade levels. Hypothesis 4 also was rejected overall from grades 2-6.

Three general conclusions based on the results of this study follow. First, children need at least three or four years of bilingual instruction before the effects of such instruction can be measured. This study shows that children who have received at least four years of bilingual instruction scored significantly higher in reading achievement than children instructed in the second language only. The review of the literature supports this conclusion. Studies involving children who have had less than three years of bilingual instruction generally have shown little evidence that bilingual instruction is more effective than monolingual second-language instruction.

Second, the data analyzed showed a definite pattern in English-reading development. Second-grade-level children introduced to initial reading in Navajo were behind the children introduced to reading in English. Third- and fourth-grade children who had been introduced to reading in Navajo in first grade were equal to or ahead of children introduced to reading in English in first grade. Fifth- and sixth-grade children who had been introduced to reading in Navajo in first grade were significantly ahead of the children introduced to reading in English in first grade.

Finally, the data indicates that the effects of bilingual instruction are cumulative. Children taught in a bilingual curriculum were behind children taught in a monolingual curriculum at the second-grade level. Children in bilingual instruction scored equal to or better than the children in a monolingual curriculum at the third- and fourth-grade levels. Each year thereafter, these children continued to score better than the children in a monolingual program. The difference in the two groups is generally greater each additional year after third grade.

REFERENCES

Campbell, Donald T., and Stanley, Julian C. *Experimental and Quasi-Experimental Designs for Research.* Chicago: Rand McNally College Publishing Company, 1966.

Division of Education, Navajo Tribe. *Strengthening Navajo Education.* Albuquerque: Modern Printing Company, 1973.

Spolsky, Bernard. *Navajo Language Maintenance III: Accessibility of School and Town as a Factor in Language Shift.* U.S., Educational Resources Information Center, ERIC ED 059 808, 1971.

_____, and Holm, Wayne. *Literacy in the Vernacular: The Case of Navajo.* U.S., Educational Resources Information Center, ERIC ED 048 584, 1971.

"The Stanford Achievement Test Results, 1972." (A memorandum circulated to all BIA schools, Navajo Area Office Bureau of Indian Affairs, Window Rock, Arizona, June 9, 1973).

Stanford Research Report, Stanford Achievement Test. New York: Harcourt Brace Jovanovich, Inc., 1973.

U.S., Commission on Civil Rights. *A Better Chance to Learn: Bilingual-Bicultural Education.* Publication No. 51. Washington, D.C.: May 1975.

A Status Survey of Texas Bilingual-Bicultural Education Programs

Ernesto Zamora

Semifinalist, Outstanding Dissertations
National Advisory Council on Bilingual Education

Degree conferred August 1977
University of Texas at Austin
Austin, Texas

Dissertation Committee:
George Blanco, *Chair*
Theodore Andersson
John Bordie
Arturo Luis Gutiérrez
Paul G. Liberty, Jr.

About the Author

Dr. Ernesto Zamora is currently an education consultant in the division of Bilingual Education of the Texas Education Agency. Dr. Zamora studied Spanish and French at Texas A & I University and Texas Tech University; he earned his doctoral degree in Curriculum and Instruction, with a specialization in bilingual bicultural education, at the University of Texas at Austin. Dr. Zamora has had experience as a classroom teacher in the Texas public schools, Texas Tech University, and the University of Texas at Austin. He also has experience as a translator/interpreter and instructor of the French, Khmer, and Spanish languages.

ABSTRACT

The purpose of this study was fourfold:

1. to utilize the literature and other documentary or interview techniques to construct a historical overview of bilingual-bicultural education (BBE) in Texas as background information;
2. to examine the literature for current information relative to what *should* be happening in BBE;
3. to obtain descriptive process information from a sample of Texas school districts to determine what *is* happening in BBE;
4. to utilize this descriptive information to generate trends and conclusions.

Efficient and effective BBE programs embrace the five basic organizational components of management, instruction, parental-community involvement, staff development, and materials development/acquisition. All too often only one or two of these components are implemented. Some of the districts surveyed have "good practices" and others have "promising practices" in one or two of the five basic organizational components. However, knowledge and change are needed at the local level on the part of administrators and teaching personnel, with strong parental and community support, before surveyed programs embrace all components into an efficient and effective model.

STATEMENT OF THE PROBLEM

In recent years the term *accountability* as a concept in educational circles has reflected a public concern to enhance the effectiveness and efficiency of public educational systems. No longer are funding authorities, lawmakers, and taxpayers asking for a cursory count of heads and resources. But concern is more pronounced for answers to questions focusing on the performance (product obtained) in comparison to the promises (resources utilized) (Tye 1971). At a time when the education profession faces tighter budgets, decreasing enrollments, declining academic standards and student achievement, a tempting thought would be to turn a deaf ear to the poignant call for accountability in education. Further compounding the ever-pressing problems is an echoing cry for equal educational opportunities via a dual-language program for all ethnic-minority-group children. This cry for equitable education both instructionally (i.e., in the use of human and material resources) and academically (i.e., with demonstrated achievement) has surfaced within the last decade.

BBE has definitely experienced its share of questions and criticism as it approaches the end of a decade of federal support under Title VII, Elementary Secondary Education Act (ESEA). While the number of these Title VII projects has steadily increased, evaluation of them has lagged behind. In the course of these years, local education agencies have made concerted but frustrated efforts to evaluate their BBE programs with inadequate instrumentation. But BBE opponents and even naive proponents have all too often released distorted, incomplete, and sketchy evaluation reports. Millions of dollars have been expended and a plethora of evaluation reports has been submitted to funding agents, yet useful, meaningful information regarding program designs, approaches, methods, or techniques is lacking (U.S. Department of HEW 1973; U.S. Commision on Civil Rights 1975; Ramírez et al. 1975; U.S. General Accounting Office 1976). This void is far from being filled, and evaluation must be improved particularly in this age of accountability as it seeks to provide timely and relevant data at all levels of the decision-making process. The reasons for failure—whether they are due to insufficient emphasis on the development of an organizational philosophy, lack of definitive policies and procedures, faulty implementation, poor curriculum design, mismanagement, or a lack of top-level administrator's support—should all be documented and reported.

In preparation for the federal "watchdogs" peering into the BBE business, a collective commitment on the part of teachers, school administrators, local and state school boards, state education agencies, and legislatures is necessary. All are responsible for making decisions at their respective levels, and all should be held accountable for the results of those decisions. An important suggestion is for the public to provide moral, financial, and active support in the formulation of educational goals and objectives and in the identification of programs to suit their needs (Browder 1971). Indications are that with continued economic, political, and social pressures, the word *accountability* will make itself heard more often and be more visible on the educational scene, thus requiring the design of sounder evaluation plans. To do this, all educators must have a more acute awareness of what constitutes a BBE program. In these programs we should be beyond the "asking why" stage (i.e., the need for BBE education), even though the needs are not yet generally known. To increase the educator's understanding of the needs of LESA (limited English-speaking ability) children and how to best meet those needs, BBE must be clearly defined as well as carefully organized and implemented (Cortada 1975). In addition, there needs to be careful and comprehensive evaluation of BBE.

Since the implementation of the Bilingual Education Act of 1968, interest, programs, and funds have increased gradually. Likewise, state lawmakers have cautiously responded to growing concern for and interest in the education of the pupil of limited English-speaking ability by enacting permissive and/or mandatory laws on BBE. Nevertheless, diverse myths, misconceptions, misinformation, and unresolved questions in the area of BBE are rampant. Educators and laypeople alike continue to seek an understandable and practical interpretation of BBE.

PURPOSE OF THE STUDY

In the present study, this investigator surveyed and described BBE programs of selected Texas public school districts in light of five major components: instruction, management, staff development, parental/community involvement, and materials development/acquisition. Emphasis is on instruction, program organizational variables, design and content, minimum characteristics, definitions, curriculum models, and typologies or taxonomies. Through a systematic descriptive-survey method of research of current conditions and practices of BBE in Texas, it is anticipated that the data and information described will facilitate the development and implementation of BBE program instructional models suitable for different locations, foster the design of improved research and evaluation activities in BBE, and provide information about BBE in Texas for decision-making purposes at the local level.

Hopefully, this effort will provide information that will create a better understanding of BBE, its basic philosophies, methods, techniques, and curriculum designs, and a better understanding of such terms as *bilingual, bicultural, bilingual-bicultural,* and *bilingual-multicultural education.* Furthermore, since this study is exploratory and descriptive in nature, it seeks to provide insights about the status of BBE in Texas, define the necessary elements for a program to be in compliance with state and federal guidelines, and list the basic variables for successful program implementation on which state education agency officials and lawmakers base decisions.

QUESTIONS OF THE STUDY

- To what extent is the BBE program being afforded guidance and leadership in terms of management and evaluation?
- To what extent are the basic instructional characteristics (Texas State Board of Education Policies and Administrative Procedures for Bilingual Programs) essential to a BBE program being implemented?

- To what extent are parents/community aware of and involved in the BBE program?
- To what extent are school administrators, teachers, and teacher aides being afforded ongoing in-service training regarding BBE?
- To what extent are bilingual-bicultural instructional materials being developed or acquired?

DEFINITION OF TERMS

In this study, the two languages of instruction will be Spanish and English. The key terms are defined as follows:

- *Bilingual education* recognizes, accepts, and promotes two languages as media for instruction, but makes provision within the instruction for understanding and appreciation of only *one* culture, in this case Anglo (see "bilingual-bicultural education").
- *Bicultural education* recognizes, accepts, and promotes two cultural foundations as media for instruction, but makes no necessary provision for instruction in more than one language (see "bilingual-bicultural education").
- *Bilingual-bicultural education* recognizes, accepts, and promotes the two languages and cultures represented. A dual-language instructional program consists of the following necessary characteristics:
  1. The basic concepts initiating the child into the school environment are taught in the language he brings from home.
  2. Language development (listening, speaking, reading, and writing) is provided in the child's dominant and second languages.
  3. Subject matter and concepts are taught in the child's dominant and second languages.
  4. Specific attention is given to develop in the child a positive identity with his cultural heritage, self-assurance, and confidence.
  (TEA, Statewide Design, 1971; State Board of Education Policies and Administrative Procedures, 1975)

Note: A "bilingual education" without the bicultural component and a "bicultural education" without the bilingual component do not contain the minimum essentials above and are *not* in conformance with Title VII, ESEA, and the state law on a program of BBE. Both "bilingual-bicultural education" and "bilingual-multicultural education" are appropriate terms to describe the above minimums.

- *Bilingual-multicultural education* recognizes, accepts, and promotes two languages and all cultures represented (see "bilingual-bicultural education").
- *Instructional component* includes the teaching personnel; the bilingual curriculum; the target pupils; the instructional methods, techniques, and approaches; and the context.
- *Management component* includes the tasks and responsibilities of program administrators/managers to systematize the other four components into a comprehensive working endeavor that will facilitate the attainment of goals and objectives. (Accountability through evaluation is a responsibility of management.)
- *Parental/community involvement component* includes the involvement (e.g., in instructional and noninstructional activities) of parents and community groups in the planning of and participation in the program. (A further goal is an understanding on the part of all parents of the program's purposes and processes.)
- *Staff-development component* includes preservice and inservice training necessary for all staff involved to understand and assure the attainment of administrative and instructional goals/objectives of the program. (This training is generally made available to administrators, teachers, and paraprofessionals.)
- *Materials development/acquisition* includes the identification, acquisition, and development or adaptation of materials for use in the program components of instruction, management, staff development, and parental/community involvement.

THEORETICAL FRAMEWORK

It would be folly to deny that BBE issues and terms need to be clarified, that disagreements need to be reconciled, and that numerous questions need to be resolved by research and evaluation. Indeed, there is an almost insatiable desire on the part of skeptics to determine if this relatively novel concept of BBE "works." In other words, what impact is BBE having on the academic achievement of children of LESA? Unfortunately, too often "weak" evaluation practices are utilized in attempting to answer this ever-present question. And part of the problem can be attributed to the fact that evaluation reports and studies on BBE programs deal primarily, if not totally, with student outcomes ("product" or summative evaluation). Often ignored is a formative evaluation, noted here as a "process" evaluation, of the happenings from program beginning to end in the component areas of instruction, management, staff development, parental/community involvement, and materials development/acquisition—all having applicability with regard to student outcomes. For example, an evaluation of program processes might view the instructional setting in terms of implementation, methods and techniques used, sequencing of materials, amount of program time, language usage (in the language arts and subject areas), and teacher-pupil interaction, among others. It is the contention of the present writer that, before product outcomes can be effectively and validly assessed, there should be a comprehensive study of the variables in the five aforementioned components. Those variables that are manageable, operational, and have a direct relationship to student performance should be considered in the evaluation process. Product evaluation should be an outgrowth of process-evaluation data collected over a period of time, not an end in itself. Without a strong process evaluation, one won't know what the product really means. An ongoing evaluation facilitates diagnosis of problems and prescribes solutions before the product is adversely affected. Suffice it to say that BBE programs should not be judged ineffective because of low student achievement without recognizing the real obstacles to success, as for example: implementation problems; mismanagement; haphazard planning and evaluation practices; far-reaching goals and unattainable, immeasurable objectives; conflicting philosophies of program overseers; lack of appropriate instrumentation; and an insufficient number of adequately trained bilingual school personnel, to mention but a few.

In order to provide a more comprehensive view of the problem at hand, the literature search includes definitions of terms, identifies myths and misconceptions, and describes and illustrates (schematically and graphically wherever necessary) both hypothetical and operative curriculum models, designs, taxonomies, typologies, or paradigms found in the literature search. This search in terms of the instructional component (organizational elements, etc.) provides the necessary conceptual framework for the present study. Models that are realistically operational and practical for implementation and in consonance with federal and state of Texas guidelines are described. The other four components will be treated briefly in light of their function in the organization of a comprehensive BBE program.

OVERVIEW OF GENERAL PROCEDURES

To accomplish the objectives of the study, the descriptive research method was utilized. The procedures undertaken were the following:

1. Tracing historical developments (1918 to present) at four levels—the legislature, the State Board of Education, the Texas Education Agency, and the local education agency—leading to the implementation of BBE programs in Texas.
2. Describing theoretical and operational views on BBE programs in the literature of experts, school practitioners, and funding authorities.
3. Querying directors/coordinators of selected Texas school districts (N=50) operating BBE programs in 1975-76 through a descriptive-survey method of research.
4. Responding to five questions of the study and reporting trends and conclusions based on information gleaned from a structured thirty-three item mail questionnaire, supplemented by secondary sources such as state and federal documents, personal experience, surveys, and on-site visits.

Of special interest in this study were responses to questionnaire items in the instructional component specifically dealing with six basic organizational features: the type of program being implemented; the amount of program time; language usage; staffing patterns; grouping patterns; and one-way or two-way patterns.

The survey data were gathered on the aforementioned components (with emphasis on instruction), processed by computer, and reported in tabular and graphic form using frequencies, percentages, and measures of central tendency. The mail-out questionnaire served as the primary data-collection technique, with secondary techniques used to check for validity and reliability.

MAIN FINDINGS AND CONCLUSIONS

The numerous hindrances to Texas BBE programs include political, social, economic, and psychological ones, to mention only a few. In the final analysis, numerous districts operating such programs are in critical need of reassessing their management and evaluation capabilities, philosophies, goals/objectives, instructional designs, community planning, parent input, staff training, and materials-development/acquisition components. These areas collectively, not a fragmentation thereof, have a potential academic bearing on the student. It does not appear that the federal or state directives in themselves, regardless of whether they are properly or improperly carried out, can effect significant changes in the quality of BBE in Texas. The passing of time and a coordinated effort from institutions (e.g., lawmakers, funding authorities, colleges and universities, education service centers, and local districts) at all levels are necessary to achieve a better understanding of the goals and promises of the concept and to increase knowledge about its proper implementation. Responsiveness on the part of parents and community groups through their support and demands can also be instrumental as the concept continues to acquire legitimacy.

While there has been a notable change in the attitude of educators and the general public over the past decade, it is apparent that it will be a number of years before the Spanish language is maintained and nurtured in the school curriculum. Attitudinal changes appear to be necessary by non-Spanish and Spanish speakers alike. The community must insist that Spanish be permanently utilized with formality and consistency in all curriculum areas and throughout a child's school years in order to maintain oral and reading competence.

There is a dearth of information on different aspects of BBE, but it is encouraging to note that significant strides have been made thanks to the efforts of specialists such as Mackey, Ulibarrí, Gaarder, Andersson, and Fishman, to mention the more influential writers. The bilingual taxonomies and typologies currently available that embrace sociolinguistic factors, student characteristics, educational goals, languages of instruction (time and treatment), etc., are excellent references for redesigning the course of present BBE programs and designing that of future ones. The responsibility lies with the program overseers, evaluators, supervisors, and classroom teachers to avail themselves of the existing corpus of information on BBE in the pursuit of new insights into the education of LESA children. Federal and state officials must be prepared not only to advise districts of noncompliance, but also to assist them in launching a program that is compatible with local needs and capabilities.

REFERENCES

Browder, L. H., ed. *Emerging Patterns of Administrative Accountability.* Berkeley, California: McCutchan, 1971.

Cortada, Rafael L. *Education for a Complex World: A Rationale and Model for Bilingual Bicultural Education.* Paper presented at the Symposium on Bilingual/Bicultural Education: Effects on the Language, Individual, and Society, El Paso, Texas, June 14, 1975. ERIC ED 110 203.

Ramírez, M., III, et al. *Spanish-English Bilingual Education in the United States: Current Issues, Resources, and Recommended Funding Priorities for Research.* National Institute of Education Contract No. NIE-C-74-0151. East Santa Cruz, California: Systems and Evaluations in Education, 1975.

Texas Education Agency. *A Statewide Design for Bilingual Education.* Austin: 1971.

Texas State Board of Education. *State Board of Education Policies and Administrative Procedures for Bilingual Education Programs.* Austin: 1975.

Troike, Rudolph C., and Modiano, Nancy, eds. *Proceedings of the First Inter-American Conference on Bilingual Education.* Arlington, Virginia: Center for Applied Linguistics, 1975.

Tye, Kenneth A. "Educational Accountability in an Era of Change." In *Emerging Patterns of Administrative Accountability,* edited by Lesley H. Browder, Jr., pp. 456-75. Berkeley, California: McCutchen, 1971.

U. S., Commission on Civil Rights. *A Better Chance to Learn: Bilingual-Bicultural Education.* Publication No. 51. Washington, D. C.: May 1975.

U. S., Department of Health, Education, and Welfare, Office of Education. *A Process Evaluation of the Bilingual Education Program, Title VII, Elementary and Secondary Act.* Vol. 1. Prepared by Development Associates, Inc., for the U.S. Office of Education, 1973.

U. S., General Accounting Office. "Bilingual Education: An Unmet Need." A report to the Congress by the Comptroller General of the United States, May 19, 1976.